Get a Job

Expert Tips on How to Write CVs, Find Employment and Win at Interviews

By Max Dobres & Mark Hennessy

Copyright Notice

This book is copyright material and must not be copied, reproduced, transferred, distributed, leased, licensed or publicly performed or used in any way except as specifically permitted in writing by the publishers, as allowed under the terms and conditions under which it was purchased or as strictly permitted by applicable copyright law. Any unauthorised distribution or use of this text may be a direct infringement of the author's and publisher's rights and those responsible may be liable in law accordingly.
Version 1.5P

ISBN-13:
978-1477612958

ISBN-10:
1477612955

Published by Bookham Consulting Associates
www.bookhamconsulting.com

In association with Objective Professional Services
www.objectiveps.com

Copyright © 2012 by Max Dobres & Mark Hennessy
Max Dobres & Mark Hennessy have asserted their rights under the Copyright, Designs and Patents Act 1988 to be identified as the authors of this work.
This book is sold subject to the condition that it shall not, by way of trade or otherwise, be lent, resold, hired out, or otherwise circulated without the publisher's prior consent in any form of binding or cover other than that in which it is published and without a similar condition, including this condition, being imposed on the subsequent purchaser.

Contents

Introduction 1

Know yourself 5

Writing your CV 23

Organise yourself to get a job 45

Where to find a job 62

Research 84

Make compelling job applications 99

Interview well 108

Ten interview questions you must be able to answer 124

Questions interviewees should ask 143

Manage the recruitment process 153

Money and the package 170

Closing thoughts 189

About the authors 191

Introduction

'You can't always get what you want, but if you try sometimes you might find you get what you need'
Mick Jagger

Two explorers are in the jungle when they suddenly see a tiger stalking them. The first explorer dives into his rucksack and digs out a pair of running shoes and starts to put them on. His explorer friend looks at him incredulously and says 'you will never outrun the tiger!' The first explorer replies, 'I don't want to, I only want to outrun you!'

Finding a job is a competition. Particularly in times of depressed economic activity and increased unemployment there will be competition for jobs. To get a job you need to out-compete all the other job seekers who are after the same jobs as you. Depending on your skills and the ebb and flow of the economy, you may face competition from a few people or hundreds. Yet in the grimmest of times there are always some job seekers who find jobs quickly or even get multiple job offers. They will be in this happy position because they have out-competed others. The ease of getting a new job is subject to many factors some of which you cannot change, but some you can. Using the right techniques everyone can dramatically improve their chances of getting a job and making sure that it is the job they want.

The authors of this book have sifted through thousands of applications and CVs and conducted hundreds of interviews.

Introduction

They have seen the passive approach taken by most candidates, but watched in admiration as a few take action and make an impact. The advice in this book is based on real experiences with real candidates. We point out the pitfalls that unsuccessful candidates fall into and tell you of the positive steps that successful candidates take to get real jobs.

This book has been written as an action-oriented, practical guide to get you to where you want to be. It is designed to give you an unfair advantage. We do not pretend to cover every issue, give every theory or investigate every nuance that may affect different skills and professions. This is a book that will guide you through the process, inspire some new ideas and give you a fresh perspective on how to compete in the jobs market.

We originally wanted 101 tips in 10 neat chapters, but life isn't neat so we ended up with 104 tips, pieces of advice and rules in 11 chapters.

Overall, the book will drive you to real, tangible and productive activity and this ethos leads us directly to our first piece of advice:

1. Be proactive.

You will not get a job by being passive. Even if you are directly approached (headhunted) you still need to put in effort to actually get a job offer. Well-directed activity is essential to your success. If you are proactive you will benefit by:

-Filling your prospect funnel with opportunities
-Having more opportunities which lead to more choice, better odds and more scope to identify the best role for you
-Be better able to measure incremental success
-Feel better about the job hunt by having clear goals, milestones and plans and knowing that each day you are taking action to get you closer to a job
- Applying the information in this book to your actual experience and becoming an expert on job hunting
-Feeling in control of the job hunt rather than being a victim of the process

Let's put it in stark terms: if you are out of work with no wage coming in, your savings will be depleted at a very fast rate. If you have a job but want a better one, the opportunity cost of delaying a move could be huge in lost earnings or slower career progression. If you need to move, be proactive; make it happen because the alternative is expensive and depressing.

Proactive means having a plan, having defined tasks and targets for achievement and taking action each day to meet those goals. Targets can be set against all kinds of activity from researching a specific number of companies, getting interviews etc.: the key is to make sure that each target you set is achievable but a stretch and will get you a step closer to getting

Introduction

a job. Many job seekers think that they are not in control, that others will determine if they get a job or not. They do not have a structured plan, are not as proactive as they can be and will prevaricate. If you avoid this trap you are already a major step ahead in the competitive stakes. BE PROACTIVE!

This book can be read cover to cover in a very short time. Every tip is a call to action; every tip is a tried and tested technique or piece of advice. Read the book and use it as a reference source for inspiration throughout your job search and you will have a competitive edge. Ultimately, your job search is entirely in your own hands, you cannot rely on anyone doing it for you. Nothing in this book is difficult and most people should be able to master most of the techniques in a short time. Most people will already, unknowingly, be practising some of what we are suggesting but even these people will certainly find fresh ideas and inspiration here.

Happy job hunting............

Know yourself

'The unexamined life is not worth living' Socrates

When you are applying for a job you must match your strengths against the needs of the job and be aware of any areas where you may fall short of the job requirements. To do this well you must first systematically analyse your abilities and then get your findings validated by others. If you do this, you will maximise the impact of your good points and increase your chances of impressing employers and getting the job.

Employers see the recruitment process as a way to find the best candidates for jobs they need to fill. The employers are trying to understand what value you will bring to them. They want to know you, but do you know yourself?

You may believe you know yourself but, when did you last undertake a thorough fact-based analysis of your strengths, weaknesses, likes and dislikes? In particular, when did you find out these things, document them, consider them from an employer's perspective and use the output to plan a career move?

The output from such an exercise we will call a Personal Profile. It is a statement of your strengths and differentiations – what makes you unique and competitive as a human being and employee based on evidence. The process of gathering this information will give you the insight you need to better plan your career, provide you with information to improve the

Know Yourself

impact of your CV and arm you with fresh facts and anecdotes that will improve your performance at interview.

Finding a job is a competitive process; to differentiate yourself it is critical that you formally gather, collate and analyse information about what your strengths and weaknesses are. This information is essential for writing a powerful and differentiated CV, effectively answering interview questions and guiding you in your job and career choices.

2. Be honest with yourself

Few of us have an accurate view of ourselves, we may see ourselves as strong in something we are really only average at, but at the same time may underrate our abilities in other areas.

If you are lucky (or unlucky enough) to read other people's CVs, you will see opening statements espousing their virtues; statements such as seasoned professional, team player, key contributor are used so often that they lose their impact. The person we know best in the world is ourselves but we judge ourselves against the world as we see it and the experiences that we, uniquely, have gone through. Sometimes we judge ourselves too harshly and fail to acknowledge important skills that we have.

We will get a more independent perspective if we judge ourselves as others see and experience us. When applying for a job, employers will base their assessment on their perception of you. This will be based on information you provide and the experience they have of you in meetings, telephone conversations and interviews. Their perception is reality and in the context of applying for a job is more important than your opinion of yourself. They make the decision to hire or not hire you so it is essential that you really understand what your strengths, weaknesses, skills and differentiations are, supported by impartial, dispassionate evidence.

Without clearly understanding who and what you are and importantly, how others see you, you cannot make rational decisions about what jobs you are suitable for and how competitive you are likely to be in securing a good role.

This chapter suggests a number of techniques and methods to gather information and analyse feedback. Use this information to build a picture of your attributes, skills, strengths and weaknesses, don't look at yourself through rose-tinted spectacles – employers won't! But don't fail to mention strengths either. Gain evidence, get facts and try to validate feedback as fairly as possible. If you know yourself, you will be much more effective in your job hunt.

3. Think like an employer, look for evidence

Employers do the hiring. They make the decisions and your role is to provide useful, honest information that assists employers to make the right choice and increase the chance that they hire you. If you can't persuade a prospective employer of your merits it doesn't really matter if you see yourself as a rising star of the business world; the employers' opinion ultimately matters more than yours.

When you analyse yourself, try and put yourself in the shoes of an employer; try and understand what they are looking for and how this matches your attributes. Use their language and terminology. You can find plenty of evidence about how an employer looks at and assesses employees in the detail of a job description or other information on the work environment which is often published on websites of larger companies.

Employers will read many CVs containing unsubstantiated claims from candidates; what they want to see are provable facts that help them make hiring decisions. Going through a personal analysis exercise will give you the facts to substantiate claims made at interview or in your CV.

So, when you are analysing your skills, personality and talents make sure you gather proof regarding your skills, talents and abilities. Make life easy for the hirer by providing proof points and evidence; this will differentiate you and will help to get that job. Many great candidates have failed to secure the jobs they wanted because the interviewers could not get enough facts and evidence to make a safe decision. When hiring it is often

Know Yourself

the case that if an employer is in doubt about a candidate – they will not hire them. It's up to you to make your case.

Understand that employers need to find people who will fit both their culture and contribute effectively in specific roles. They will look for a mix of skills and behaviours and will have a language to describe what they are looking for. If you can put yourself in an employer's shoes and really understand what they are after and how they would recognise it then you have given yourself a huge advantage in competing for a job.

4. Describe yourself in employers' language

We are all a different mix of strengths, weaknesses, strange behaviours, motivations and fears. These attributes are shaped by our unique life experiences, training and interactions. It is difficult to find a way of describing accurately and in a way that others can understand who and what we are and therefore we need to describe human characteristics in a language that employers are familiar with.

Below is a list of attributes and skills that covers most of what you need to measure for your personal analysis but there are no hard and fast rules (apart from being honest with yourself) so if you wish to add categories, feel free. For each category collect a specific piece of evidence that demonstrates your performance on an attribute and score yourself from 1 to 10, where 1 is for a very low ability and 10 for very high; try and measure at a consistent level and don't be too generous in the scoring! Fair is more useful than flattery! However do consider all of your experience and pick out examples that show you at your best. For example, under problem solving, two people might both rate themselves as an '8', one choosing scheduling a particularly complex project as evidence while another describes how they arbitrated between two colleagues who disagreed. Both are problem solving but they bring out the different ways they might be expressed in different individuals. Most importantly however, both have evidence to support the rating of '8'.

Under job-specific skills add specific skills and experiences that are required for your job or profession.

Know Yourself

Attribute
Intelligence
Problem solving
Tenacity
Team working
Concentration
Numeracy
Written skills
Verbal skills
People oriented
Organisational skills
Analytical
Multi-tasking skills

Job-specific skills
-To be added by you (such as specific job-related skills like programming languages, experience of specific equipment, profession-specific skills etc.)

5. Gather your evidence

The first step is to write down a comprehensive list of your strengths and weaknesses focussing on the attributes discussed above such as intelligence, flexibility, work ethic, people skills etc.; you can then move on to more specific job-related skills.

Now find supporting evidence for both strengths and weaknesses – ideally more than one piece of evidence for each attribute. Write all of this down to make it easy to review.

After you have undertaken the self-analysis exercise, cross-reference this with previous reviews or appraisals from your employers (if you have them). Employer appraisals are rarely perfect records of a person's abilities and skills (frequently they are generous in praise and light on criticism) but they will give a useful cross-check to validate the information you have collated.

Now look at your successes and failures in your work history; has your career progression been fast or slow against your peers, what tasks did your employer give you, did you tend to work alone or as part of a team? By looking at what has happened in the past you will get some evidence that will assist in validating your self-analysis. Write down specific examples as evidence of these abilities.

Look for specific achievements you can quantify. Numbers imply greater accuracy. For example a project manager might say that 17 out of the 18 projects they managed came in better than 95% of cost and time budget and the 18th was on budget.

Know Yourself

If you understand how others view you, you gain a deeper understanding of your true skills and abilities. This enables you to best present yourself, understanding what traits may be obvious to someone else and which may need extra emphasis. Self-analysis is the first step in gaining this understanding. Having undertaken this you can then seek information from people you have known or have worked with and this will further validate and add to the understanding you have of yourself.

6. Get feedback from people who know you

First you need to work out whose opinion will be valuable, impartial and informed. A good selection of people to seek opinions from would be a manager, a peer and someone who has worked for you. If you have worked in a customer-facing role and you can get one of your customers to give an opinion that would also be very useful. Conversely, if your roles have been more internally focussed, find out from colleagues what their opinions of you are. Do not rely only on the opinions of those who you were most friendly with as they may find it difficult to give you balanced or negative feedback.

Explain to them that you are asking these questions to prepare for a review and that they can help you most by being honest. Tell them also that it will be useful if they can give specific examples of things you did or said and what the effect of this was. This will guide them away from broad opinions and give you specific evidence you can use.

You can use your previously prepared self-analysis to provide a structure to the conversation but do not allow this to provide leading questions or influence the output you receive.

Ask open questions that look for general strengths and weaknesses and then seek more specific job-related information. Always get supporting evidence; if the person says you are a natural leader, ask for a real example that would illustrate this behaviour. Try to be neutral and do not react to the information and answers you receive and do your best not to ask leading questions that are only seeking flattery. It is

Know Yourself

essential to take written notes ideally during the conversation so that your brain is not tempted to filter the feedback in any way.

7. Write a Personal Profile from the analysis

Once you have gathered all the information, recorded the evidence and validated the information as much as you can, you need to commit it to paper.

You are aiming to create a written Personal Profile of your achievements, abilities, motivations and what work environments and cultures best suit you as a person, together with the evidence to support it. You do not need to write the most elegant prose as this profile is a working document for you and not meant for public consumption.

From the attributes we have suggested and you have added, try writing under each heading how you perform, where your strengths and weaknesses are and under what circumstances you may excel at a given attribute. What you write should not be unduly positive or critical but a balanced, factual statement written with an understanding as to how an employer would perceive you. Each point should be supported by a factual example.

The written Personal Profile is your permanent reference point and reminder of who and what you are from a skills and work attributes perspective. By committing this complicated information to paper, it allows you to see through your own propaganda and look at yourself as others (and particularly, employers) see you. By understanding this you have the ability to choose what you can do more accurately, discount things you are not suited to and understand where you have special abilities and advantages that can make you a more competitive

Know Yourself

candidate. It is also a useful reference point for future self-improvement.

You can also use this analysis to pinpoint any development needs that require more experience, development or training. You might for example take a short course in using computers, or look for opportunities to improve public speaking skills.

The profile also gives you great source material to help you write a targeted and effective CV and is particularly useful in creating the introductory personal summary on your CV.

8. Use your Personal Profile to target jobs

Your Personal Profile should give you a clear and substantiated view of who and what you are. It will identify your core attributes and you will be able to cross-reference this with jobs to understand where you may be competitive in gaining a new role.

When you look at different jobs and careers you will see that they require different skills and attributes. Clearly many jobs need specific job-related skills and some jobs and careers can have a very high barrier to entry due to large amounts of these specific skills. As an example, a brain surgeon needs a steady hand and an ability to concentrate for long periods – similar attributes to a watchmaker or tailor but you would not want anyone who has not had many years training taking a scalpel to your brain! The brain surgeon will have many years of detailed medical training and therefore their role is not easily transferable to people not trained in these specifics. But many jobs and careers have significant overlap with others jobs and careers; experience in one may mean the opportunity to apply your skills in a new area is much easier than you think – it's your task to persuade the employer!

When you went through the process of creating your Personal Profile, you broke down your capabilities into defined skills and attributes. With some practice, you can disassemble jobs and make a fairly accurate guess as to what each job will need in attributes and skills. Written job specifications from employers or recruitment companies are often good at describing job-specific skills but with some thought and analysis, you can get a deeper understanding of what they are really after.

Here are examples of jobs that share similar attributes where a person could potentially move between them.

Personnel Officer, Recruitment Consultant, Personal Counsellor, Office Manager, Personal Assistant
(key attributes are a strong people orientation, empathy, communication skills etc.)

Car Mechanic, Technical Sales, Mechanical Apprenticeship Trainer
(key attributes are an understanding of mechanical systems, a common vocabulary and ability to communicate effectively)

Call Centre Operative, Retail Sales, Radio Presenter
(self-confidence, verbal communication skills)

Actor, Sales Executive, Motivational Trainer
(self-motivated, confident, self-starter)

Writer, Journalist, Bid Manager, Website Content Manager
(written communication skills, attention to detail, empathy with the reader)

Musician, Software Engineer, Business Analyst
(able to handle complex structured and unstructured information, analytical, collaborative)

9. Use the Personal Profile before interviews

Having researched and prepared your Personal Profile you will have looked in depth at your historical strengths, weaknesses, triumphs and failures and have evidence to support it. All of this information will be fresh in your mind and will provide the factual basis for delivering great performances at interview.

Before an interview you should study the role specification you have been given and spend time researching the company. This research will give you strong clues about the attributes required for the role and general behaviours that succeed within the company. Use this research to prepare, noting facts and anecdotes from your Personal Profile to provide substantiated answers for questions that might arise.

Interviewer question: Are you a team player?
You: Yes, as an example in 2009, I was asked to turn around a failing team where low morale was a key issue. I delayed the implementation of my initial strategy in order to listen to the team's issues and on the basis of this modified my original plans to incorporate some very positive ideas. I encouraged two team members to lead work streams and for a period of time I worked for one of these individuals to deliver some of their additional ideas. As a result of this, the team improved performance, staff turnover decreased and the team was recognised by senior management for their improved contribution.

Your Personal Profile brings into sharp focus your capabilities, strengths and weaknesses. An employer is trying to find out the same things at an interview. When using your personal statement as a guide to answering interview questions it helps you to focus not just on what you did but also answer the implied 'why' and 'how' and what were the results? By using your Personal Profile as a reference point you have an opportunity to sell yourself more effectively because of your deeper and better understanding of an employer's perspective. Your use of evidence will make your claims much more credible.

By having a thorough understanding of yourself, not only can you sell yourself to an employer more effectively but you are also able to explain in much greater detail why the job is right for you. Remember that when employers hire, they will always look favourably at people who really want (or need) a particular role. Understanding your own analysis will enable you to communicate, in a clear and compelling way, why the role fits/suits you.

Writing your CV

'O would some power the giftie gie us to see ourselves as others see us' Robert Burns

CV stands for Curriculum Vitae, a summary of academic and professional history and achievements. The CV is your sales document enabling you to showcase your talents and demonstrate your suitability for a specific role. A CV is often used during job interviews to help frame questions and guide the structure of the interview. A CV must therefore achieve a good balance between being differentiated and strong on impact and having factual information clearly laid out in the right (expected) order and format.

Your CV is a critical document. It is usually the first significant way an employer or recruiter gets to know about you. Their time is short and you must make a quick impact or your application can be doomed. There has been much written on how to write the best CV. In reality, there is probably no best way but there are many wrong ways. The following tips will help you create a strong CV for most purposes and avoid most of the common mistakes. Your CV should not go anywhere without its constant friend the covering letter.
CV is more correctly abbreviated as C.V. but for ease of reading we have gone with CV.

10. Assemble your facts

The CV is a document that should communicate to a potential employer

    a. What you have done
    b. When you have done it
    c. How you have done it
    d. Why you have done it
    e. With whom have you done it!
    f. What impact or benefit you had to the organisation.

Accepted CV formats, styles and conventions vary across different countries but the most common convention requires that you provide your career experiences in reverse chronological order.

You will need accurate information on the following:

-Details of current and previous employment with dates to the nearest month as to when you started and when you left. If there are periods in your career where you have had a number of very short-term roles it is acceptable to lump them together with a description and explanation – see example in tip 17.

-You will also need accurate information on your qualifications: where and what you studied and what qualifications you were awarded.

-Your salary and benefits information (not usually put on a CV but essential to know for your job search).

Employers may ask for proof of information on your CV and omissions or mistakes will generally be judged very poorly. As part of the information-gathering exercise find your exam certificates, historic offer letters, P60s and payslips and put them in a safe and accessible place.

It is strongly recommended that you gather all relevant dates and information on all employment and qualifications even down to the most distant seemingly unimportant thing. You may not actually put everything on your CV but you need to know in case you are asked – it can look bad if you have forgotten something you have done or are inaccurate with how you describe it.

11. Write a personal summary

Write a personal summary that briefly describes what you can do and why you would make a great employee. It should be one or two paragraphs long, no more than 100 words.

The personal summary breathes life into your CV; without it, the CV would just be a list of what you have done and give an employer no way of understanding who you really are.

In chapter 1 we discussed how you would put together a written personal summary that describes you and your abilities as a person and future employee. The personal statement on your CV is a concise benefit-oriented version of this; its purpose is to provide an easy-to-read quick 'sell' of who you are and why an employer should hire you.

The personal summary is your chance to make an impact. It is normally placed at the front of a CV and should be one of the first things an employer will read. Most people do a fairly poor job of selling themselves at this stage because they write too many subjective and unsupported statements:
Example:

I am a popular, honest and hard-working individual who has strong organisational skills. I have strong people-management abilities and lead from the front.

When a recruiter sees a statement like this they will think to themselves 'says who?' It is better to support your statements on character and skills with facts:

I am a popular, honest and hard-working individual who has strong organisational skills. Selected achievements include:
-Out of 300 employees, I was voted employee of the quarter Q1 2009
-In 2008 I led a £500,000 project to move offices and despite being let down by the removals firm my personal intervention meant that we completed the work on time and below budget
-I initiated and led a cost-saving exercise that changed work practices across 3 departments and saved my employer £4,000 p.a.

When supported by facts, personal statements about your character and behaviours come alive and are no longer just your opinion. These examples also show how to weave the impact or benefit your actions had into the summary. In the last example the employer will immediately think maybe this person could save me thousands of pounds per year too.

Use the FAB structure: Feature, Advantage and Benefit where:
-Feature is a fact about you
-Advantage says what this means
-Benefit is the 'So what' to the hiring company

Writing your CV

12. Name and describe your employers

Virtually all CVs list the names of employers but this is not enough, you must also describe who those companies are and what they do. Most hiring decisions at some point need to take into account the sorts of companies and therefore the sorts of cultures and environments you have previously worked in. You should not assume that because you have heard of a company that others will know who they are. When describing the firm you can describe some facts that bring out their strengths and differentiation.

Examples:

Fred's Insurance Agents June 2008 – Present

A leading Insurance Agent firm servicing the Blackpool region and specialising in corporate insurance for small businesses.

Ace Telecom July 2005 – August 2009

Ace operates on 5 continents and 200 countries worldwide and is a leading global provider of integrated information and communication solutions to meet complex customer needs.

Recruiters will make judgements about you depending on where you have worked. You cannot assume that everyone knows the companies you have worked for.

13. Structure your CV

Your CV needs to follow certain structural rules so that information can be found easily.

Those involved in recruitment may need to read tens or sometimes hundreds of CVs. Most CVs will not be fully read, they will only be scanned for key information to allow the recruiter to count you in or out. If information cannot be found easily most people will not have the patience or time to read your CV so you will be rejected.

The structure should be as follows:

1. Name and contact details

2. Personal information*

3. Summary/Introduction – your personal summary (including a description of the type of role you are seeking)

4. Jobs (and sabbaticals etc.) in reverse chronological order

5. Education in reverse chronological order (including training courses)

6. Additional Information including hobbies and interests

7. References

   * It is not usually necessary or required to put your age or date of birth on a CV

14. References

References are often overlooked, yet can act as a very powerful sales tool even before they are taken up.

A large proportion of people work within specific industries and tend to move between firms in the industry they have experience in – if you are an estate agent, you are likely to try and find a job in another estate agent. Industries tend to have a circulation of people from one firm to another and therefore some senior people get very well known. When you ask people to be referees for you, you should try and get the most senior and best-known people to agree to do this.

If you get a well-known and senior person to be a referee for you, and give their name, company and job title (with contact details to be supplied on request), future employers will be impressed that such a well-known figure supports you.

Don'ts

Don't ask someone who barely knows you.

Don't put someone as a reference if you have not gained their permission.

Only ask people who you are fairly sure will have good things to say about you.

Do not put referee's contact details on the CV – you must have control over access to them.

Dos

Use references relevant to your work.

Get the most senior person you can.

Ask their permission first and make sure they will be around when you need them.

Have backup referees in case you need references for multiple jobs or your first choice referee is away.

15. Look and feel of the CV

Your CV is your sales document. It needs to look and feel professional and easy to read.

a. Not too long and not too short. See Tip 17.
b. The typeface needs to convey the right image. Experiment with different fonts and styles before you decide.
c. White space is OK, don't crowd the words together, it can discourage the reader.
d. Use bullet points. Few CVs are read word for word all the way through so the document should be laid out so that the key information is easy to see and the bits that you wish to highlight are positioned in such a way that they are seen.

When designing the CV remember who you will be trying to impress. If you are applying for a graphic design job then your CV's look and feel could be a little more elaborate with creative use of design techniques – this approach could have a negative impact if you were applying for a job as an accountant or a lawyer as a more conventional approach in these professions may be better received.

There are CV templates available with Microsoft Office and Word and also others available on the Web and these can be a huge help in getting a reasonable looking CV produced quickly. If using a template, ensure it has the flexibility to include all the information you want to include and the end result looks good; get friends or colleagues to give an opinion.

If you are using Microsoft Word to create your CV, you may want to experiment with saving the document in a PDF format as this often creates a more professional visual appearance and prevents anyone editing it without your permission.

Your CV is your sales document. A recruiter will typically see your CV before they see you. If it looks ugly, scruffy or difficult to read it dramatically reduces your chances of being invited for an interview.

16. Check, check and check again

Your CV needs to be as good as it can be. You need to check every word very carefully and when you have gone boss-eyed looking at it, get a friend to check it as a fresh pair of eyes can often spot things that you cannot.

Spellcheck the CV, but remember that spell checkers are not perfect and may miss some errors. Make sure you use the correct spellchecker for your country; US spellings are often different to British spellings! A good example of a common mistake is:

'I was a Principle Consultant' when what is meant is 'I was a Principal Consultant'.

One additional tip: if you design your CV on an Apple computer using Apple software, email your CV to someone with a PC and Microsoft software so that they can review the format. It is common that the CV will arrive in a different format – usually wrongly sized. It is an easy mistake (and a very common one); a CV viewed at 150% sizing looks ugly and is not the first impression you want to make.

Inaccuracies, spelling mistakes or major omissions in your CV will reflect badly on you. Inaccuracies will invariably be uncovered through the interview process or referencing; getting it fixed early is by far the best strategy.

17. How long should my CV be?

Not too long and not too short! There is no perfect answer but some good guidelines are:

-The more senior you are the longer the CV can be. A rule of thumb is one to one and a half pages for someone at the beginning or early stages of their career and three pages for someone more senior.

-A CV should be long enough to communicate concisely an overview of what you have done and how you have done it through your career but should not include too much detail – it will rapidly become boring to everyone apart from you.

-It is unlikely that a CV (even for someone starting out on their career) is less than one page.

-It is unlikely that any CV needs to be longer than four pages, remembering that there should always be lots of white space. Generally, employers are more interested in things you have done in your more recent past – maybe five years or so – and your distant past is of less detailed relevance to a hiring decision. If you have lots of jobs early in your career you can group them to save space and include less detail.

Writing your CV

18. Sample CV

The following sample CV demonstrates good clarity of design and format as well as clear delivery of information. Although this example covers many pages in this book it is three pages long when formatted as US letter or A4 size.

Fred Smith
20 The Close
Sheffield
Berkshire
RS16 9DD
Home   01189 56789

Office   0282 45678

PROFILE

A Senior Customer Support Director experienced in setting up and managing successful customer support operations for systems and software suppliers. Committed to the achievement of high customer satisfaction making use of extensive experience in technical support, quality management and customer account management. An enthusiastic and effective leader with a proven ability to motivate and organise a team to achieve results.

CAREER HISTORY

Noddy Corporation PLC (acquired by Big Systems) 2001 – Present

Director Customer Service, EMEA

Noddy Corporation is the leading supplier of metal products to the building industry. It has a turnover of c£100m and offices across Europe and the US.

I Joined Noddy Corporation in January 2001 reporting to the VP of Global Support, responsible for all aspects of the support business and service delivery in EMEA with 35 staff, an expense budget of $3m and revenues of $27m. In August 2010 Noddy was acquired by Big Systems PLC. Long-term position within Noddy still to be determined at present.

Achievements to date include:

- exceeding revenue targets for H1 2001 despite a 20% reduction in renewals base revenue through removal of an international uplift charge;
- forming and growing a new management team for Customer Support in EMEA;
- significantly improving global linkages and consistency;

Writing your CV

- improved customer satisfaction levels, particularly for Enterprise customers through the creation of a critical situations function.

CDW Corporation   1994 – 2000

One of the most innovative and successful global software providers in the industry with a turnover of over $1.2Bn. Acquired by XYZ in June 1997 as a wholly owned subsidiary.

Senior Director, Worldwide Support Centre Operations, 2000
Promoted to this position on 1st January 2000, I was responsible for all of CDW Customer Support Centres globally reporting to the VP Technical Support and Engineering.

Responsibilities included:

- managing an organisation of over 600 people globally through a management team of 6 regional directors and/or site managers and 2 global function heads;
- managing a global operation with expense budgets of circa $50m and revenues in excess of $60m;
- increasing global consistency and quality of CDW support services.

Achievements included:

- reduced support costs by 3% annually while improving customer satisfaction in 5 out of six years;
- led major change programme in North America to restructure support delivery;
- built new global support management team.

Support Operations Director (Europe, Middle East and Africa) 1997 – 1999
Promoted to this position on 1st November 1997, I was responsible for the Customer Support Centres in Europe located in UK, France and Germany. Dual reporting to the VP of Global Customer Support and the EMEA VP of Professional Services.

Responsibilities included:

- managing an organisation of 170 people through a management team of 3 support centre managers and 3 European wide function heads;
- managing support operations with an expense budget of circa $20m and revenues in excess of $30m;
- delivering increased customer loyalty to CDW products and services through the provision of high quality, cost-effective support services.

Achievements included:

- led an industry award-winning change management initiative in EMEA which moved the organisation from being product centric to customer centric;
- improved customer satisfaction ratings across Europe by 17 percentage points in an 18 month period with a doubling of 'very satisfied' customer ratings over the same time period;
- increased margin contribution by $2.5m over an 18 month period;
- led the consolidation of 3 support centres in EMEA into a single large centre located in Dublin resulting in $4m savings;
- shortlisted for 'EMEA Manager of the year' in 1997 and 'Worldwide Manager of the year' in 1998.

Customer Support Centre Manager, Northern Europe
Initially hired in 1994 as Communications Support Manager for various products, I was promoted in January 1995 to manage the Customer Support Centre for Northern Europe based in Birmingham. Dual reporting to the General Manager of Customer Support for Europe, Middle East and Africa (EMEA) and the UK Managing Director.

Responsibilities included:

- managing an organisation of 74 staff through a management team of 7 line managers;
- managing a support centre with an expense budget of $5.5m and revenues of $7m; delivery of technical support services including, first-line telephone support, second-line technical support, field support and technical account management, for all products, to customers and Business Partners in UK, Ireland and Nordic countries;

Writing your CV

- actively participating in the general management of the UK company by sitting on the UK management team.

Achievements included:

- increased customer satisfaction ratings for communications product support by a factor of 2 over a two year period;
- reduced staff turnover from 50% to 7% over a two year period;
- grew support revenues by 200% while controlling expenses at 16% growth over a two year period;
- achieved ISO 9001 certification for the quality management system implemented in the support centre;
- awarded 'Services Manager of the Year' in 1995.

Software Ltd   **1989 – 1993**

An international software and services company owned by GRT. UK turnover £9M; 70 employees.

Technical Support Manager
Initially hired as Communications Support Team Leader and within 18 months promoted to Technical Support Manager. I was responsible for managing all aspects of the delivery of a high quality technical support service to over 7,000 users across 25 customer sites through a team of 8 support staff.

XIR Systems UK   **1988 – 1989**

An international Canadian-owned supplier of office systems hardware, software and systems integration services, previously known as SDF Data. UK turnover £20M; 200 employees.

Networking Manager, Sales Support
Responsible for leading a team of networking and communications technical specialists engaged in producing technical sales proposals and conducting customer demonstrations and presentations. I was instrumental in securing a number of contracts by successfully managing a number of major 'proofs of concept' and implementation projects at key corporate customer sites.

DRT Group   **1984 – 1988**

Services Team Leader, DRT Network Systems   1987 – 1988

Assigned to the head office of DRT Network Systems to recruit and set up a team of engineers to support the management information requirements of over 200 internal users.

Quality Assistant, DRT Development   **1986 – 1987**
Responsible for the design and maintenance of a quality management system for a software development group producing open systems networking software for DRT large- and mid-range systems.

Software Support Engineer, DRT Network Systems 1984 – 1986
Part of a team responsible for providing technical support for an open systems networking product.

EDUCATION
   BSc (Hons) in Electrical and Electronic Engineering 2.1 Queen's University Belfast

   11 'O' Levels plus 3 'A' Levels
   Mathematics   Grade A
                                                              Further
Mathematics   Grade B
                                                              Physics

PERSONAL DETAILS

Marital status: Married with 2 daughters aged 9 and 2.

Interests: Golf, Cooking and Entertaining, Natural History, Politics

19. Keep your CV up to date and relevant

Your CV is like your will; it is an important document that needs to be kept safe (in PC terms that means backed up) and it needs to be kept updated. Therefore, when you complete a significant piece of work or achieve something exceptional, add it to your CV but make sure you keep an eye on the overall content and level of detail so that your CV doesn't become bloated.

Immediately after any interview where you have used your CV, think about improvements that may have made the CV a better document and make the revisions quickly while the thoughts are fresh. As suggested below you may want different versions of your CV for different jobs

If you have multiple versions of your CV, ensure they are all updated simultaneously so that the different documents don't start to diverge too much on content.

20. CV security

If you have gone to great effort to produce a fantastic document that portrays you exactly as you wish, you should save the document so that unauthorised people cannot change it. It is a simple task with most document authoring packages such as Microsoft Word and will avoid unscrupulous recruiters customising your CV without your knowledge.

Better still, Word and other packages allow you to save your document in PDF format that reduces the risk of it being changed and minimises the chances of it looking different on different computer systems.

Many recruitment agencies will routinely make changes to CVs to put your details into their standard format or to highlight your suitability for a specific role.

Mostly these changes are for benign reasons but by having your CV distributed with 'Read Only' protection, you retain the editorial decisions!

21. Have multiple versions of your CV

Most people have multiple talents and broad experience enabling them to consider a number of different jobs or roles. It is a good idea to have a small number of CV versions that emphasise different skills, strengths or experiences related to different job types. The versions do not need to be radically different; you might just need to change some bullet points to include different experiences or change the order of things.

You can then refine your CV depending on the job you are applying for, for example if you have a background in retailing and you are applying for a job as a salesperson, you will emphasise your selling abilities and achievements, whereas if you are applying for a buying job you may want to put more emphasis on brand awareness and merchandising skills.

By doing this, you can have CV versions specifically suited to different types of roles and maximise your chance of standing out from the crowd and getting the interview.

Organise yourself to get a job

'Eighty percent of success is showing up' Woody Allen

You must look upon the job hunt as an exciting opportunity to get a new job. However the reality of the job hunt can get you down if you approach it in the wrong way with the wrong expectations. Right at the start you must tell yourself that this could be a long process, it could take six months or more. If you have only defined success as getting a job, then you are facing a lot of disappointments. This can wear anyone down.

Organise yourself to get a job

22. Set manageable goals

Recognise that a job hunt may take a long time and to set smaller goals that measure incremental progress along the way. You must also recognise that you may have to identify 60 to 100 opportunities before you get one that turns into a job. That sounds a lot, but if you break it down over an initial 12-week period that just means finding 5 to 8 opportunities a week.

So that is how you approach hunting for a job; you take an initial period, say 12 weeks and you give yourself goals. Goals like this:

End of week 1: Identify 10 opportunities.

End of week 2: Have applied for 10 opportunities and found 6 more.

-
-

End of Month 1: Identified a total of 24 jobs, made 18 applications and had 4 interviews.

We suggest that you set goals for periods of at least two weeks.

Every four weeks review your goals and add another four weeks' worth of goals so you are always looking at a 12-week rolling period.

23. Celebrate your successes

If at the end of month 1 you have indeed identified 24 jobs, made 18 applications and had 4 interviews that is a great achievement, even if you have not found a job yet. You have achieved your interim goals. Reward yourself with a treat; it could just be a half-day off job hunting.

The key to all processes such as this job hunt is perseverance and it's difficult to keep going without celebrating milestones.

If you keep going and are applying for jobs you can do in the right way then you will be successful. The fact that you only apply for jobs you can do and you need to find five to eight new job opportunities each week will push you to look in new places. Use the section on proven places to find jobs to make sure you are searching thoroughly and not missing any opportunities.

24. Make failure your friend

You will not get the vast majority of jobs you apply for. No one does. However, each time you get a rejection letter or just don't hear back it can feel bad, but it's not; it's a chance to improve and it creates a new job opportunity. You learn little from success in any field, but you learn lots from failure. When you don't get the job you can ask yourself, why not? Maybe you made a mistake, your covering letter was not good, the application was late or you said something you regretted in an interview.

Each week it is important to think through what has happened in the previous week and try and use it to improve each aspect of your application.

Better still, ask the organisation that rejected you – 'why?' You may not be able to get to talk to everyone you applied to but make sure you talk to some of them. Very few people go back to the recruiter and ask why they didn't get the job. You need to do this and to listen rather than become defensive. You could make a phone call to get the feedback but it's better if it's a face-to-face meeting. You say to them:

'Thank you for the opportunity for applying for the job as a "Manager" (or whatever) with your company. It was good experience and the process was well run. I'd be really grateful for some candid feedback on what I did well and what I could have done better.'

Then you listen; you don't get defensive, they aren't going to change their mind. What they are giving you is their view of how you seemed to them. It is their reality. Listen to it and use it to improve your technique.

But you can snatch a future victory from the jaws of defeat. Your next question is:

'I was really impressed by your company, are there any other opportunities you have that you think I might be right for?'

If they say no you say:

'Would you mind if I called you in about four weeks' time to see if anything has changed.'

You then make sure you do call in four weeks' time and every four weeks after that. After each call you send a very brief email thanking them for their time, reminding them in a brief paragraph who you are and saying you will call again next month.

You have now created your own personal channel to finding new jobs before they are advertised.

You may think you are being an irritating person who won't take no for an answer, they will think you are committed and persistent and stick with a task until it gets done. Just what every employer wants.

25. Treat getting a job as a sales process

You must treat the process of looking for a job as a sales process. Most job applicants are too passive; they are victims of the recruitment process. You need to build a plan to get a job. The core of the plan will be a 'job funnel'. A job funnel is a list of all the job opportunities you are working on listed according to the probability that you will get the job. The least likely are those that you have just heard of, the most likely are the ones where you have got further, perhaps an interview. You classify all your jobs into categories like this:

Suspect: (0%)
This is a job you could do and have the experience and qualifications for.
Action: Apply for the job.

Qualified Prospect (20%)
You have applied and your application has been accepted.
Action: Understand the next steps.

Developed (40%)
You have submitted an application and have a first meeting or interview scheduled.
Action: Attend a meeting or interview and talk through your CV with the recruiter.

Proposed (50%)
You have completed one or more meetings and those you have met agree you can do the job.
Action: Understand what each of them is looking for. Record and deal with any objections.

Selected (60%)
The decision maker has verbally told you that you have the job, subject to agreeing terms, getting references and signing an employment contract.
Action: Review the job offer and make sure you have agreed pay and conditions and that your referees respond.

Won (80%)
Receive a formal job offer from the employer with salary, start date and employment contract.
Action: Return all documents to the hiring organisation and check that references have been received.

Committed (95%)
Your signed offer letter and contract received by employer, start date confirmed.
Action: Turn up and start on time.

You should then use a spreadsheet to track each job, recording the job details, its progress using the above categories, next actions with dates and other comments.

Organise yourself to get a job

Organise your life to get a job

Finding a job will be your job until you have secured a new position. Unless you set aside time, have a routine and take the process seriously, there is a strong chance that things will move slower and be less effective than needed. Every week without a wage can amount to a lot of lost cash; every week in the wrong job is opportunities lost. Failure to take job hunting seriously is a very expensive option!

The process is started by adding 'suspects' at the entry to your list of opportunities or 'job funnel'. These suspects are then moved through the process by applying the right tasks. If you have enough quality suspects and process them well, you will achieve your job objective. The process is also self-correcting. As you go through and move your suspects to later stages or eliminate them, you will learn what works and what does not work.

Plan your day to work through your opportunities and move them down the job funnel. In most cases you will need around 60 opportunities to get one offer. Plan your first 12 weeks. The table below gives an indication of how you will spread your time in hours per week.

Hours spent per week

Week	1	2	3	4	5	6	7	8	9	10	11	12
Plan & Review	18	2	2	2	2	2	2	2	2	2	2	2
Add Suspects	2	12	6	3	3	3	3	3	3	3	3	3
Qualify		6	6	3	3	3	3	3	3	3	3	3
Develop			6	6	6	6	6	6	4	4	4	4
Get short listed				6	6	6	6	6	4	4	3	3
Get selected									4	4	3	3
Win											2	2
Total	20	20	20	20	20	20	20	20	20	20	20	20

Notice that in week one you will spend most of your time planning, but as you progress you will always spend at least two hours per week on planning and review. This is based on 20 hours a week which also allows time for you to do part-time work, be a consultant or work as a volunteer, all of which, as described later, will enhance your chances of getting a full-time job.

In the first few weeks you will spend a lot of time adding suspects, by week four onwards this task will still occupy around seven hours per week. One of the biggest failings of novice salespeople is that they generate good suspects and then throw themselves into qualifying them and moving them further along the pipeline. Unless they are very lucky this batch of suspects does not lead to sufficient business, but since new suspect generation has been neglected, the cupboard is bare and they must start again.

In the job hunt, things can go wrong at the last minute. That job negotiation you thought was going so well suddenly stalls, a

Organise yourself to get a job

new candidate enters the frame or there is a hiring freeze. Without a full balanced funnel, you too will waste valuable time.

The basic process you will follow is to move suspects through the pipeline until they either disappear or turn into a job offer.

26. Know what job you want

It is likely that your skill-set and your aspirations mean that there is more than one job type or role you can go for. It is unlikely that you will have more than three or four job types although there may be many similar roles that fit within these major job areas (also be aware that different companies may use different terminology to describe the same roles).

You may be an HR specialist and your main target might be to get a job as an HR Executive or manager in the HR department of a company. However you might also consider becoming an HR consultant working for a consulting company that specialises in advising companies on such matters. Finally you may be interested in going freelance and offering your services to several small companies as an external HR specialist.

For each of these write down the following details:

Organise yourself to get a job

Job title(s)

Write down the most common job titles associated with this job.

Main Responsibilities (Objectives/Outcomes)

Think about the job from an employer's point of view. How does this job add value to the company?

Main Activities (What is done most of the time)

Critical Success Factors (What must be done well)

Employing Organisations

Department Head Titles

Salary Required

27. Only apply for jobs you can do

Once you are clear what types of jobs you want and have organised yourself to feed the opportunities funnel, ensure you make best use of your time by only applying for jobs where your skills and experience match that sought by the employer. Advertised and online job adverts in particular get swamped by unqualified applicants vainly hoping that the recruiter will set aside the needs of the job and see some special quality in them.

Well, it isn't going to happen. When your CV gets to a company an administrator compares it against a list of criteria and if your CV doesn't match, the application is rejected. Submitting applications that get rejected because they don't match the job criteria is a waste of your time. It may feel like progress because you've applied, but it isn't.

So if the job advertisement says they are looking for someone with five years experience in retailing and you have three years experience as a postman, forget it. You may have great people skills and be very enthusiastic and even love shopping, but if you don't have a reasonable match to the experience asked for you will not get past the first stage.

The corollary to that is if you are applying for the job and you do have the skills and experience, make sure that it is very clear from your CV and covering letter. In particular make sure that you use the same words as they do. So if the job asks for three years of telesales experience and you have it, use those words, do not say 'inside Sales' or 'Telemarketing' or 'Customer Relations Management'. If they say they want sales experience and you have it say so in their terms. Otherwise the administrator doing the CV sifting may reject you unnecessarily.

28. Decide if you are prepared to move house

Be clear in advance about where you can work. In particular be clear about which areas you can commute to and which areas you would need to relocate to.

For areas to which you can commute to, be clear about the time and cost of commuting. Take the time to research the costs of rail travel and frequency of services to major centres of employment near you. If you would commute by car, make sure you know the true cost of commuting, including parking costs and the time it would take in the rush hour to make the journey.

If you need to relocate, make sure you have thought this through in detail and discussed it in advance with your family and others who might be affected. Do not worry about this if and when it happens, worry about it now! It is a complete waste of time to apply for a job and get it, only to decide later that moving is impractical.

If you are prepared to move and you think it likely; then do some basic research on house prices, schools etc. for major centres of employment.

Be clear on how easy it will be to sell your house and move and think through how you would handle a three to six month period in temporary accommodation or a very long commute.

Be clear also whether you can afford to fund the house move yourself. When doing your calculations, remember stamp duty, removals, estate agent fees and all the other myriad costs that are associated with a move. Some employers only pay relocation expenses for existing employees and few employers will cover the total cost of a move. If you might need help with relocation, then ask right at the start. That will give your employer the chance to decide what to do. Some companies require additional levels of approval if relocation is to be part of the package. This may not be a problem if it is raised and resolved in advance. If you wait until the end of the recruitment process to raise it you risk boxing your employer into a corner and getting a refusal for something that might have been agreed with more time for consideration.

Another option is to not move but to live away from home during the week and commuting on a Monday and Friday. If being away from your loved ones during the week will not break your heart then this is a less disruptive option. You need to factor in the costs of accommodation, food and sundries. Hotels are not the only option, there are many less expensive ways to live away such as B&B, self-catering furnished accommodation and rent a room schemes.

29. Look in the right place

By all means apply for jobs advertised online and in newspapers, but to be successful you must go beyond that. This is explained in more detail in the next section but the key points are worth repeating here.

Very few jobs get filled through being publically advertised. Most jobs are never advertised. Often this is because suitable candidates insert themselves into the job hunt process before this can happen and they get considered first. Your task is to be one of these proactive people. Most candidates will not do this. If you do, then you greatly increase the odds of getting a job simply by cutting out most of the competition. Depending on which queue you want to jump, there are various techniques and these are explained in later chapters.

For now you must recognise that the conventional approach to job hunting is inadequate and that you must do more with the hidden opportunities to get yourself a job fast. An active approach recognises that there are a large number of different access points where job opportunities are to be found and puts in place an action plan to attack them. Job advertisements and listings are the easiest to find, but they are also the avenues that attract most competition. All the other sources of opportunities take more effort to identify, are more painful to find, but once found yield better job opportunities.

30. Share the pain

Looking for a job is hard, if you can find someone to share the load with this it will help. Ideally it could be a fellow job hunter. If you can find someone like you who is also looking for a job, then set up a regular meeting, ideally once a week, where you can share ideas and measure progress against your plan.

Try and agree on a common approach to looking for jobs like the sales process, goal setting and time management described earlier. That way when you meet you will have specifics to discuss, how many new opportunities, interviews and so forth.

Treat the meeting like an informal business meeting. Have an agenda covering the topics you want to cover and set a time limit for the meeting. Keep it positive and focussed on how you are each doing compared to your plan; the goals you have met and the lessons you have learned. Congratulate each other on success and celebrate joint achievements. Do not let it degenerate into a mutual bitching session where you complain about how difficult and unfair it all is.

If you can't find another job searcher then a friend or partner will do, but it will help if you clearly explain the purpose of the meeting and limit the time so they know what is expected of them and how long it will take.

Where to find a job

'Choose a job you like and you will never have to work a day of your life' Confucius

There are many obvious places to look for a job such as advertisements and online listings. However these places only account for a minority of all jobs available. However, this is where most people look. Not surprisingly these jobs have the most competition and are the hardest to get. You should, of course, apply for these jobs, but in this section we will tell you how to find the majority of jobs that don't get advertised and attract far fewer applicants, ideally just you.

In this section you will look at some of the key 'routes to market' and how best to maximise your ability to find and develop the largest number of relevant opportunities. Finding a job can be a little like trying to fill a leaky bucket with water; many of your applications will be rejected or fail at the interview stage but as long as you are generating fresh opportunities there is a good chance you will secure a fantastic role. Too many people when looking for a job use only a small number of routes to market and as a result limit the volume and quality of opportunities they identify and hamper their ability to make the best decisions.

Different roles and industries will have variations on how they make use of various routes to market. High-tech jobs will generally be at the forefront of using the Internet and social networking sites (or indeed innovations we have not even thought of yet) while other industries may major on the use of recruitment agencies or in-house recruiting teams. It is important to understand that in almost all circumstances there will be multiple places and methods to find the job you are looking for. Trial and error and experience will help you to understand the dynamics of your target industry and different routes to a job. Experiment and measure results and you will quickly become proficient at navigating multiple channels and routes to finding a new role or career.

31. Never rely on a single route

There are many potential routes to finding a job and technology is accelerating the trend by adding new ways of communicating. Many candidates will rely on a single method to find a job such as using recruitment agencies or applying via online advertisements. This approach may work reasonably well in an economy where there are a large number of roles on offer but in more difficult times it will be harder. Having multiple channels gives you more choice, increases the chance of you finding the best available role and also gives you more opportunity.

Evaluate and use some or all of these routes:
- Your network – people you know or people who know people you know
- Direct applications – identify and research companies and go direct to them
- Recruitment companies – both national chains and specialists
- Online advertisements
- Press advertisements
- Job fairs
- Company websites
- Social/business networking sites – such as LinkedIn, Facebook, Craigslist etc.
- Volunteering
- Consulting or temporary work
- Industry events

Finding a job, particularly during an economic downturn, is largely about out-competing other job hunters. You must assume that every job you find and every job you apply for will have dozens or more people chasing the same role.

By managing multiple routes to finding a job you can improve your market knowledge; you will increase the volume of roles you identify and if you are well organised you will be able to react quickly to opportunities. If you rely on one route to jobs – say using recruitment companies, you lose access to many roles that are not being filled through that channel and you lose control of your ability to compete to your best advantage.

32. Get the best from a recruitment agency

You would assume that recruitment companies would always do their best for you as they generally get paid only when they find you a job. This is not necessarily the case for a number of reasons:
- A. They get paid for filling jobs and will fill the easiest roles with the obvious candidates first.
- B. They are human and subject to the same laziness, incompetence and other weaknesses that affect us all.
- C. They are usually overwhelmed with large volumes of candidates and therefore the chances of them being able to really look after your interests in a proactive manner are small.
- D. Recruitment companies are generally paid by employers and not candidates therefore their motivations will be biased towards looking after clients more than candidates.

In the developed world recruitment companies are a major route to finding and securing a new job. There are thousands of recruitment firms covering every conceivable market sector and they potentially offer a very efficient way to get access to job opportunities that will best suit you. They aggregate huge numbers of jobs and make it easier to get the right candidates in touch with the right employers. They are a critical and valuable resource for the job hunter to use but there are tricks to getting recruiters to do their very best for you.

Make a friend of a recruiter so that they see you as a human being. When a recruiter spends his or her life looking at thousands of CVs it can be easy to forget that real people lie behind the CVs. Address this by always speaking with the recruiter – ideally before you even send your CV; telephone them, explain who you are and promise to follow up once your CV has been received. Get to know them and let them get to know you; wherever possible meet them in person for an interview. Once you have met a recruiter you have a great opportunity to impress them, sell to them and make them understand that they can potentially make money out of you; they may even see you as a real human being!

Make life easy for them. Ensure your CV is easy to read with information clearly presented. Ideally tailor your CV or covering letter to address, point for point, the requirements of any specific role you may be applying for. Most recruitment firms will use PC-based recruitment software packages that can electronically read CVs and spot key words to aid the finding and shortlisting of candidates from their databases. Remember this and ensure that your CV uses language and terminology that is standard and recognised for your industry.

Keep in touch with recruiters without being too intrusive – try and understand how often the recruiter would like to speak with you and don't exceed this otherwise you will have a negative impact.

Give the recruiter clear guidance that will help identify the role you really want.

Try and identify recruiters who have good market knowledge and a good attitude to service; it is worth investing time to

Where to find a job

cultivate good recruiters for the long term as they may be very useful in developing your long-term career.

Be reliable, if a recruiter asks for a revised CV by a set date; make sure you hit that date. Never, ever, miss or be late for an interview arranged by a recruiter. If you make them look bad to their client they can lose future business. Let them down once and they won't take the risk again. Conversely be a good candidate and even if you don't get the first job, the recruiter will put you forward for others.

33. Make high-impact direct applications

You should make applications to companies directly without applying to a specific vacancy or using an intermediary. You do not even need to be aware that there is a vacancy available.

It may not seem to make much sense to apply blindly to a company without even knowing if they have a relevant vacancy available. However, most companies have a great deal of 'churn' as people are leaving and joining all the time. There is a good chance that they have people who have recently left or new posts that have come available but have not got round to formally advertising them yet. If your application arrives at the right time you have eliminated the competition at a stroke. It is likely that your application will have a life of four to eight weeks. So you can repeat an application every three months.

If you make an application to a firm directly, the outcomes could be as follows:
- A. They ignore you.
- B. They respond and say 'no thank you – we have no vacancies now but will consider you in the future'.
- C. Your CV lands on the desk of a decision maker on the day they decide they need to hire – bingo.
- D. Your CV lands on the desk of a decision maker and they think 'wow, this person is just what we need; I wasn't planning on hiring but let's create a role so we don't miss out on this great hire'.

The last two actions do happen. When they happen you may find yourself with no competition from other candidates and the added advantage that the hirer may think that you have more initiative than other candidates.

In previous chapters we have discussed using your Personal Profile to understand your attributes and what types of roles you can be suited for. In the next chapter you will look at research methods and how to identify companies by industry, location, business type etc. where you may have a competitive advantage.

The first step when making direct applications is to carefully select your targets and thoroughly research why they may be interested in hiring you. You are looking for what we call 'hooks'. A hook in our context is a compelling reason why a company would be interested in speaking with you and hiring you. The hook may be that they have already hired some of your ex-colleagues, you may have competed with them; you may work in the same industry. If you cannot find a hook for a particular company then they are probably not a great target for a direct application.

There are many ways of making a direct job application to a company but the most commonly used is an email application targeted to a senior executive within the company. The email should be short and to the point and clearly include the 'hook' as a compelling reason why the company should meet with you. It is important that you create a punchy, direct and easy to understand email that states why you are a great candidate, make a few well-described points as to why they should meet you and ask for a response (or even better, promise to phone/email within a week or so if you have not had a response).

An example of an email approach may be:

Dear Fred,

I am looking for a job.

I was recently working at The Acme Company, a company you may well know as we have shared a number of market segments over the years. My role within the firm was in the customer service department where I was an analyst responsible for identifying inefficiencies within customer support and creating new processes to streamline support response times and avoid some common complaint issues.

My recent major achievements have been:
-21% reduction in customer escalations beyond first-line service desk;
-12% improvement in customer complaint resolution times resulting in a direct saving of £11,000 and 6% improvement in customer retention.

Given recent press coverage of your new marketing campaign, I have no doubt that you will see an increase in customer volumes and I believe I could help you to maximise the opportunity this growth will give you.

I have attached my CV and I hope you will find it an interesting read. I am keen to meet with you or a relevant person within your organisation and will call you next Tuesday to see if there are grounds for us to meet.

I look forward to speaking with you.

Regards
John Brown

Where to find a job

34. Handling internal recruiters and HR

Many companies now employ recruiters on their payroll who are focussed on just filling jobs within their own company. You will most often encounter internal recruiters in large companies where there is a high volume of roles to fill. Internal recruiters will often handle a wider variety of roles than external recruiters and will almost certainly manage much higher volumes of roles. Internal recruiters are typically paid a base salary with a small variable component to their salary whereas external recruiters will generally have a much higher proportion of their salary dependent on commission. The volume of roles and compensation issues has significant effects on how internal recruiters operate and how you need to manage them to best effect.

Internal recruiters will typically be very process driven in their roles. The high volume of jobs they may be handling means they must be very focussed on ensuring CVs are a good fit for a particular role so it is very important that you customise your CV to clearly show how your skills fit with a particular role (if advertised) or if applying via an application form you are very clear exactly how you fit an opportunity.

There is less scope to build personal relationships with internal recruiters because they are often very busy and generally involved in CV generation and first-line filtering of CVs and not the later stages of the selection process though there are exceptions to this. You need to make it easy for them at the CV or application form stage to see, point by point, where your skills fit and why you would make a great employee.

By all means, when you apply try and telephone so that you can have an opportunity to speak in person but if you are not successful within two or three attempts, do not persist with telephoning as this may just irritate the chased recruiter and have a negative impact on your prospects for success.

35. Get the best from recruitment fairs

At recruitment fairs a number of employers get together at a single venue to meet face to face with large numbers of candidates. Often there are many employers and potentially hundreds or thousands of candidates all competing for attention in a hot and airless hotel or conference venue. It can seem daunting and difficult to make an impact with the right people.

Follow these tips and you will maximise your chance of making the right impression:
- A. Dress appropriately.
- B. Have a number of printed copies of your CV with you and ideally a copy of your CV on a USB memory stick.
- C. Do research in advance. Plan which companies you want to talk to and work out what they may need that you may have to offer. Don't spread yourself thinly by trying to talk to everyone but make an effort to impress those companies most likely to fit your aspirations and skills.
- D. Understand that employers at these events are very time pressured so make an impact, be concise, try and get commitment to follow up with a formal interview and then move on. People who talk too much do themselves no favours.
- E. Get contact details or business cards from the people you meet and follow up via email or phone a couple of days after the event.

Recruitment fairs can be a very effective way to meet companies face to face without intermediaries or technology getting in the way. Normally these fairs are either industry or geography specific and can offer a good chance to quickly get in contact with a number of potential employers. It is important to make a quick and positive impression because it is easy to get swamped by the numbers of other candidates and quickly forgotten after the event. If you plan in advance, dress to impress, make a concise but powerful impact and then follow up after the event, you will maximise your chances of success.

Where to find a job

36. Job boards

There are a large number of online job boards so you must find websites where jobs are advertised that are relevant to you. There are large national or international sites such as Monster, Jobsite and Reed that carry a huge variety of roles across different industries, job types and levels of seniority. Many national newspapers such as the *Guardian*, *Financial Times* and the *Daily Telegraph* have vacancies advertised on their websites. There are also hundreds of smaller sites that serve specific niche markets, geographies, industries, job types or levels of seniority. There are also thousands of websites that operate as the shop windows for individual recruitment companies. Many large companies will also advertise their own vacancies on their corporate websites.

Many of the job boards allow you to upload your CV to a database that can be searched by hiring companies and recruitment firms. This can be an effective way to get jobs to come to you but you must be aware of the pitfalls. Do not place your CV online if you are already employed in a role unless you do not mind your employer finding out you are looking for a job. If this is a problem you could post your CV anonymously but this could still a risk if there are clues in your CV about your identity.

Secondly, do not leave your CV on a single job board for an extended period of time (more than two months for example). If you do, employers may assume that you have had difficulty finding a role and are a less attractive candidate.

37. Make the best use of personal referrals

Many people get a job through a personal referral. This is where you know someone who either works for the firm or who is sufficiently connected to the company that they can give you privileged access to the decision makers and vouch for you. This personal connection can significantly increase your chances of landing the role.

The advantages of personal referrals are many. Firstly, it is a great way to minimise competition. Where an application in response to an advertisement may pitch you against hundreds of other candidates, as a personal referral, you will face very few competitors and you will have an endorsement from a current employee. Internal referrals can be a short cut to a shortlist of one!

Many companies (particularly larger ones) operate 'internal referral schemes'. The scheme encourages employees to refer people they know as potential employees and offer payments, bonuses or other rewards to the people who refer people who are subsequently employed. Companies do this because internal referrals can be very cost-effective hires. In theory, the candidates are already part-selected for their suitability and because there are no recruitment company fees or advertising costs they are very good value from a company perspective.

The secret of internal referrals is to find someone who is willing to refer you. In previous chapters we have looked at the importance of undertaking thorough planning and research for

Where to find a job

your job search. Part of this research is defining your network of people you know and the organisations they work for. You need to be able to identify people who will have connections into companies that you are qualified for and interested in working for. Usually they would be current employees of the target company but they may have other links to the firm such as being personal friends with employees or being a supplier to the firm.

Once you have identified your target referrer, you need to find out if there are relevant vacancies available; this can be done through searching a company's website. If you do not find evidence of a vacancy, do not be dismayed as often roles may not be advertised. Companies may even hire people because they offer a solution to a problem rather than a planned vacancy being available. If they do have an advertised vacancy, it helps you to refine your CV, supporting letter or pitch to the referrer.

When you make your approach to the referrer, be direct and clear that you are asking them to refer you. Tell the person that you are asking for them to help you get a job at the target company. Explain the type of role you are interested in telling them briefly why you think you are relevant and then give them your CV and supporting letter. Try and get their email address so that you can provide the same in an electronic format.

While you do not want to make a nuisance of yourself, it is important that once you have made an internal referral application, you maintain gentle pressure to track and drive the process forward. Once you have made your application to the referrer, it is perfectly acceptable and advisable to contact them after a week or so if you have heard nothing; you must always remember that getting a job for you is always more important for you than anyone else – so a little chivvying along will ensure people do their best for you.

Many people find selling themselves or asking for favours difficult, imagining that people are unwilling to help or that in some way they are imposing on friends by asking for their assistance. If you do feel this way, you need to get over it! Firstly, ask yourself, would you be willing to help someone who asks for your assistance? Of course you would. Secondly, if you don't ask, you generally don't get. Thirdly, what is the worst that can happen if they cannot or will not assist (a very unlikely situation)?

38. Use networking to your advantage

Many people are intimidated by using their network for personal advantage. You may dislike asking for favours or seeming too brazen or desperate to people you know. There are ways of building and using a network that will get round these fears. You must remember that most people, if asked in the right way will generally provide a small amount of help to others but few people will give a huge amount of assistance. The secret is to ask for lots of small favours – 'can you introduce me to someone or do you know anything about this company?'

Everyone gets to know (to varying degrees) a large number of people and those people will know an even larger number of people. Let us say you know 20 people who you have worked with and each of those people knows 20 people; that equates to 20 X 20 = 400 people in your easy to reach network. In reality, most people will know more than 20 people but the maths gets more difficult. The people in your network who can be of assistance to you are the individuals with direct connections with your chosen industry or with indirect connections to it (married to someone relevant or know someone who is in the industry).

All job hunters should be signed up to social networking sites such as Facebook or LinkedIn. These sites are a good starting point to build a list of people in your network who may be of assistance to you, but you should also think about ex-colleagues, customers, suppliers or clients from your past.

Once you have defined your network and have a list of people and an approximate understanding of how they can be of assistance, you need to decide how to approach them and specifically what kind of help or assistance you are after. Meet them, call them or drop them an email, whatever you are most comfortable with. Let them know that you are looking for a new role and would value their help or advice. Do not steam in immediately asking for a two-hour face-to-face grilling where you will extract every ounce of useful knowledge they possess – this will only shut doors for you.

Your network is particularly useful for getting market intelligence, introductions to other useful contacts, access to unadvertised roles or other information that may give you the edge in your job search. When you have found your new role, do not let your network wither and die. Make sure you are available to help people in your network, pass on useful information and generally keep in touch, you never know when you may need friends or they need you.

39. Visit industry fairs and conferences

Every industry has trade fairs, conferences and exhibitions. At these events are many senior executives and a vast, publically available amount of information on the companies. Go to these events, meet people and gather information. You can make a reasonable assumption that among the people manning the stands at exhibitions are relatively senior staff: be brave, approach them, get them engaged in conversation and let them know of your interest in joining their firm.

These events are often attached to conferences and there are very busy times, during breaks, when the stands are busy, but there are also very slow times when there are hardly any people on the exhibition floor. This is your time, the company representatives are bored, have time and they're trapped on the stands.

Not many job hunters go to these types of events, so you have an immediate advantage.

When you get to meet people on a stand you must keep it short. Give them a hard copy of your CV, get their business card and promise to email your CV (for them or for forwarding to a more relevant person). Follow up with a call a week or so after the event to make sure you have not been forgotten.

40. Work as a contractor or a consultant

When you are looking for work, you want to find a job as quickly as possible to minimise the time you are not earning and to avoid the dreaded gap in your CV.

Looking for a job is hard work but it is rarely equal to a full-time permanent role. Even hard-working job seekers will rarely spend more than four hours a day productively looking for a role. With the spare time you have, get a part-time job. There are numerous opportunities to use you skills even if it is unpaid. You could offer to help train or mentor people in your industry, do freelance work, work for a charity, assist with meals on wheels etc. If you do something related to your sector, you can uncover useful inside information or position yourself as a candidate for a role. If a role is unrelated then it is still better than doing nothing.

You can offer yourself as a consultant or contract worker doing work the same or similar to the permanent job you want. The market for full- and part-time jobs can be separate so you give yourself a new pool of opportunities to go after.

Once you have a part-time job with a company, you are an insider and can more easily see what jobs are available and as an almost internal candidate might get considered early.

Research

'Time spent in reconnaissance is seldom wasted' George Smiley

Looking for a job may seem like a chore and can be an anxious time. However, it should also be looked at as an opportunity. We have spoken to many people who said that looking back, losing a job was the best thing that happened to them. It pushed them out of a role they had not really enjoyed and back to a place where they could choose what they wanted to do. The transition was painful, but worthwhile.

Finding the right job and career direction is not just important, it is vital. You live once (in this dimension and body at least) and owe it to yourself to do the best you can. This means more than maximising your cash income: it means finding something to do that is matched to your talents, interests and abilities. You spend a significant proportion of your waking hours for 40 or more years at work; if you don't own the thinking and research behind finding the right role then you are taking a grave risk with your future.

No one will work harder for you when you are looking for a job than you. By undertaking your own research, you set the pace and agenda, you gain the market knowledge and you direct activity towards opportunities that will best suit you. Finding a job and deciding exactly which opportunity is best for you are driven by access to information – if you don't have the information, you will not be able to find the best opportunities or make the best decisions.

41. Use your Personal Profile to broaden your job options

Most of us are defined partly by the job we do; we are accountants, salespeople, nurses or any other job title. Once you have completed your Personal Profile you will be able to define yourself by your core skills, abilities and motivations and not just by your job title. This different way of looking at yourself will enable you to deconstruct other jobs and careers and view them as a set of core required skills and then match your skills to roles you may not have considered before.

As an example an accountant may see his/her core skills as:
-Numerate
-Methodical
-Process and task oriented
-Individualist
-Problem solver
-Great attention to detail
-Business understanding

This set of core attributes could also lead to other roles related to accountancy such as purchasing manager, administrative manager, planning executive, managing director etc.

When you are looking for a new role, there are benefits in having as much choice as possible, it maximises your chance of securing a job but also gives you more input into your career direction. However, be realistic, the aim is to broaden your view of jobs you are qualified for by looking at the underlying skill-

Research

set. Test any conclusions by making sure you do have the core skills for any new career direction.

Some people are adept at changing careers but most people are relatively cautious. It must be noted that the more senior, specialised and expensive you are, the more difficult it is to change career *at a similar salary level.* At the early stage of a career it is easier to change career and indeed many people do try different things before they settle on a final direction but it is important to keep an open mind and flexible attitude when deciding what you can do.

42. Have a clear target, but be flexible

On an archery target the centre is gold; it's a perfect hit, but each ring scores points. So even if you miss the gold (your perfect job) getting close is okay too.

In an earlier section you defined what job you wanted, in this research phase you use that as a guide but maintain the flexibility to apply for related jobs you might not have thought of.

When you undertake research for a new role you need to decide what your priorities are and look for companies and opportunities as close to this ideal as possible.

Your priorities may be set by wanting to work locally, remain in the same industry or work for a particular size of company. Consciously start looking for companies closest to your ideal criteria and work outwards.
When searching for an opportunity you can utilise Internet searches, websites such as LinkedIn or if you are looking for a role locally, you could physically travel around the commercial centres and business parks in your area and note which companies are there. If you are looking to work in a specific industry you may want to visit some trade shows, look at the membership of trade associations or search online.

If you have a particular desire to work for a small or start-up business then it is often an idea to find one company and find out who the investors or financial backers are (information usually available on its website or in news items). Once you

Research

have found out whom the backers are there is a good likelihood that these backers have also invested in other similar companies – and so your network of knowledge will increase.

A huge proportion of job moves are from one company to a competitor, customer, supplier or company in a very similar market and most people find a job within travelling distance of their current home.

If you focus on the most likely seams of information closest to what you want and what you are best qualified for then you will make best use of your time and energies.

43. The Internet is a great source of information – use it!

Before the Internet, getting good information about companies was difficult, now anyone can easily get large amounts of detailed information about a company. There is therefore no excuse for arriving at an interview unprepared. There may also be little point in applying for jobs at a company that has just announced redundancies. Here is a list of some Internet locations worth looking at.

A. Company websites.
B. LinkedIn – the primary international business social network is a great way to find out who works where and also spot where your ex-colleagues or people in your network work.
C. Venture Capital/Private Equity firms – look at where they are investing. Where such a firm has made a recent investment, this generally means growth and hiring. They are also a useful way to look at companies in various segments as venture capital firms will tend to specialise in certain types of companies and generally advertise all previous investments on their website. Don't limit yourself to only looking at locally based companies; often investment decisions in other countries can affect hiring decisions in your area.
D. Partner organisations. If you have expertise in a specific market segment don't just consider the large companies, look at who they partner with. Large companies such as Ford, Microsoft, Rolls-Royce, British Aerospace etc. will all partner with many smaller

Research

companies that operate in complementary areas and will often list them on their website. Looking at partners can dramatically increase your market awareness and also the number of potential employer firms you can look at.

E. Financial and business news websites can be a source of information about recent company events. There are often industry or regional profiles that describe leading companies in a sector.

F. Specific Google searches can be used to uncover new opportunities. Rather than search for 'engineering companies' and get a huge unrefined list back try refining your search to specific sectors and geographic areas. For example searching for 'electrical engineering KT2' will return a specific list of companies in that postcode because it hooks into Google local and maps. Whereas searching for 'electrical engineering jobs KT2' is good, it gets you a list of jobsites, but perhaps not as useful as the former search.

44. Don't forget traditional information sources

It is a good idea to tap as many information sources as possible in order to build a rich and balanced understanding of any subject. Though the Internet has revolutionised the speed and volume of information gathering, the old methods of speaking to colleagues or reading newspapers should not be ignored as they offer a different perspective and often a more personal or up-to-date insight. Use sources such as:

A. Colleagues/network
B. National and local newspapers
C. Trade bodies
D. Recruitment companies. Niche recruitment companies can have detailed market knowledge and speaking with them can often open new opportunities or enable you to build better market understanding.

When looking for a job, knowledge is power. A central theme of this book is that you, the candidate and job hunter, take control. You must drive the search using the tools and resources at your disposal. An essential part of this empowerment is undertaking your own research, finding out information unique to your search and circumstances. The better the information you have, the better informed your decisions and actions will be.

Research

45. Know what you need to know

There are key pieces of information you need to know about a company both before deciding to make an application, when making an application and prior to interview. Research is good but you need to be sure about what key items of company information you need. These are:

A. Size – revenue and staff numbers
B. Market – what is their market from a sector and geographic perspective?
C. Products or services – what they do
D. Differentiators: how do they add more value than their competitors?
E. Challenges – what opportunities or challenges they have
F. Triumphs – what have the historic successes been?
G. Recent news – be up to date with what is happening
H. Hooks – what links you to them or their needs?
I. Financial data: recent revenue and profit figures with commentary (getting better or worse?) and share price movements if a quoted company

The more information you have on a company the better informed you will be about your suitability to them, what your competitive strengths may be and how best to get that message across. Use of this information in interviews and meetings will show you are a serious candidate. In our experience the majority of job hunters don't do this.

46. Find out about people

LinkedIn and other similar networking websites are very effective places to research business people. They have powerful search features that allow you to find current and past employees of companies or search on a number of other criteria. In addition, LinkedIn may be able to identify how you may be linked to these people – i.e. they may know someone who knows you.

When you identify a company you are interested in do a search and identify as many employees of that firm that you can. It may be possible to identify likely managers, hiring personnel, peers and influencers. You should do this research even if you are introduced to an organisation via a recruitment firm.

Remember knowledge is power! More research leads to better knowledge and a greater likelihood of identifying a hook that will be your killer advantage in getting a job. People buy people, so understanding who works for a company, what their backgrounds are, how you are linked to them and other similar information gives you huge advantages in knowing who to apply to and how best to sell yourself to them.

Research

47. Identify hooks

A hook is anything that links you or makes you interesting to the organisation or individual within it. It moves you a short way along the line from 'one of them' to 'one of us'.

As you research companies, bear in mind why you are gathering information. You are looking for market intelligence to assist you to find the companies and roles that are relevant to you and will directly assist you in finding a new job. It is also important to gather information that will assist you in selling yourself into the target company. If you think about it from an employer's perspective, they need reasons why they should hire you – we will call these reasons 'hooks' because, if they are used in the right way they will help to grab an employer's attention and help you to catch them!

The hooks need to be easily communicated reasons that assist you in explaining why an employer should consider you.

Early in the job hunting process you should have undertaken a thorough analysis of your skills, experiences and abilities; analysed your network and identified lots of things that add to your uniqueness.

When you are researching companies, you should be looking for things about that company that may prove an overlap or complement to the skills and experiences you have. Examples of what to look for are where companies operate in the same industries, markets or geographies where you have experience. You may have worked with the same customers or worked with similar business processes or challenges (such as mergers, new product launches etc.). You might find people in your network who are already employees of the business.

You can find information for identifying hooks on company websites, newspapers or other reporting that can often be easily found online. By undertaking this level of research you can develop a strong understanding of the company's business which will prove very useful at interview but most importantly it will give you ammunition to identify hooks and build a targeted and concise sales message that can be used either to make an application or during the selection process.

As you will see later you will need a few choice facts about a company to reveal at interview. This shows that you are generally interested in the company and have the initiative to find out more.

Research

48. Track & collate information

You will be collecting a great deal of information and you will not be able to remember it all so you will need to capture and record information in a structured and retrievable fashion. The information will consist of media articles and website pages, brochures and possibly verbal information given to you by recruiters or people in your network.

On your home computer, set up files for each company and record this information and try and ensure you always capture a minimum of the following:
- A. What they do
- B. How big are they?
- C. Have a reasonable understanding of the history of the organisation
- D. Financial turnover and profit
- E. Who the senior leadership team is
- F. Current employees you know
- G. What has been said about the organisation in the press over the last 12 months?

Gathering information will equip you to deal with the entire job application process, but it will not be of use unless you can retrieve it when needed.

The information you gather will enable you to:

A. Find companies that could hire you.
B. Understand the background to these companies, what they do and how they do it.
C. Understand who their competitors are.
D. Find out the strengths, weaknesses and challenges they may be facing.
E. Get some understanding as to who works at the companies you are interested in.
F. Understand what you have that they may want.
G. Formulate intelligent questions to be used at interview.
H. Demonstrate understanding, market knowledge, preparation skills and interest in a company.

Your research process is similar to preparing for an exam; you need to prepare for all eventualities but you must be selective about how you use the information. Do not attend an interview and try and impress them with the sheer quantity of information you have collected. Use your knowledge to selectively impress and demonstrate insight but not to bore the pants off a luckless interviewer.

49. Get first-hand experience of a company

Many companies sell direct to consumers or their products and services are accessible to consumers. If you are applying to a company whose product is available to buy or try, do so. Clearly you cannot buy a car or a pension just to seem informed at an interview but you could go into a car showroom and have a first-hand look at the cars prior to attending an interview with a car company or you could look at the pension products online and even engage in the early part of a sales process to buy a pension to see what the customer experience is like.

This is a great way to demonstrate interest, curiosity and commitment to a future employer. You may also get a valuable insight into the strengths and weaknesses of a company through being a customer or engaging with them as a potential customer. It is also a great way to get an understanding of the ethos and working culture of an organisation and will greatly assist you in deciding who you might be comfortable working for.

Make compelling job applications

'He who hesitates is a damned fool' Mae West

You have done a lot of hard work understanding yourself, putting together a great CV and identifying a target for a job application. An employer sees none of the effort they just see the result, so make sure that when you apply you do it with energy and in the best way you know how.

There are numerous possible ways to apply for a job such as email, telephone, in person (at a jobs fair) etc. We will not try and cover every permutation but will looking at the most common ways for applying for a role; responding to a job advert, making a direct speculative approach or going through a very structured approach where you need to complete an application form.

Make compelling job applications

50. Write application letters and emails

The vast majority of applications for a job will involve emailing or posting a copy of your CV with an accompanying letter or email message.

The secret to a great job application letter or email is to keep it short and to the point. The letter should state what you are applying for (or what type of a role you are interested in if you are making a speculative application) and give only a handful of really compelling reasons why you are the ideal candidate. If there was a reference in the job advert make sure you use it.

Dear Hiring Manager

I am applying for the role of Purchasing Manager that you advertised recently on the Monster job board reference ABCD12345.

I am extremely interested in the role. It is a good match to my skills and fits well with my career ambitions. Some of my skills and abilities that may be of particular interest are:

> *-I managed a purchasing spend of £15m for The Fred company where I identified and negotiated savings of 6% over a 3 year period.*
> *-I rationalised the supplier base from 38 down to 15 key suppliers while increasing the range of products available and shortening delivery times to 2 weeks.*

-I led a team to define and implement an upgrade of a software purchasing application which was delivered on time and to specification.
-I can offer direct purchasing experience gained in a related industry to XYZ Corp and I have a real desire to further my career in a growth-oriented organisation such as yours.

I feel confident that I have both the skills and motivation to excel in this role and I am very keen to attend an interview where I can demonstrate my suitability.

Yours sincerely

You will see that this letter embodies the FAB structure referred to earlier: Feature, Advantage and Benefit where

-Feature is a fact about you
-Advantage says what this means
-Benefit is the 'So what' to the hiring company

51. Applying for an advertised job

When applying for an advertised job make sure you thoroughly read the job advert and fully understand the requirements and how you match them. Make sure your CV and covering letter make it easy for a hiring manager to see and understand how you match the criteria for the role. Customise your CV and provide additional supporting evidence to ensure your application is as strong as possible.

Try and call the recruiter or hiring manager in advance to make personal contact. Ensure you are speaking to a decision maker rather than an assistant. Your conversation needs to be short and to the point; be ready with one or two reasons as to why you are a compelling candidate. Make sure that you establish a rapport in the short time you have on the phone as this will go a long way to establish you in the mind of the hiring manager. Do not bombard the hiring manager with lots of questions or a long monologue about why you are the greatest candidate – the quickest and surest way to get onto the reject pile is to bore or irritate the hirer.

If your reply is an email, make sure that you put the right job reference in the subject line. This is businesslike and efficient and shows the company you are well organised.

When replying by letter, use good quality paper, but beware of anything too fancy. Thick vellum will jam in the feeder of some photocopiers.

52. Making an application from cold

Where you are making a general and unsolicited application to a company you need to make sure you direct the application to the person who is best able to understand what your skills are and has the ability and authority to progress your application. The Human Resources department is rarely a good place to start. The best person to apply to is usually the head of department in the function that your skills relate to: salespeople will apply to the Sales Director, Finance people to the Chief Finance Officer and Director level candidates to the Chief Executive. You can generally get the name of the right person through research on LinkedIn, the company website or by telephoning reception and asking.

Most applications these days are via email. Email addresses are generally easy to guess and if you get it wrong, the email will usually bounce back to you. Email conventions are usually one of the following:

John.smith@webaddress.com

jsmith@webaddress.com

john_smith@webaddress.com

or .co.uk, .org, .net etc.

Before you make an unsolicited application, thoroughly research the company; understand what they do and how your skills and experience could benefit their business. Your

Make compelling job applications

application letter or email and CV should make it clear what you can offer that directly overlaps with their business for example, if you have worked in the same industry, similar processes, technologies etc. Also in the cover letter, make it clear why you wish to work for this company. The rule as always is to be concise and to the point.

Experiment with real letters hand addressed and sent by mail. The prevalence of email means that senior managers in larger corporations get very few physical letters compared to a torrent of emails. Your physical letter may increase your chances of getting noticed. This will vary by industry so try both and see which works. Include your email address in the letter so they can reply electronically if they prefer.

53. Make your application form great

Application forms reduce your ability to differentiate yourself compared to a CV. So make sure you spend extra time getting them right.

For some roles and in some industries you will be asked to fill in a standard application form instead of or as well as sending your CV.

There are a few critical tips in filling out application forms:

A. Make sure your handwriting is legible and neat and that your spellings are correct.
B. Think about and rehearse what you will write before you commit it to paper.
C. Understand precisely what the organisation does and what skills, attributes or values they require and ensure that your answers concisely demonstrate your fit to their requirements.
D. Get the application form completed and returned before the deadline date.
E. Keep a copy so that you can remember what you wrote.
F. If you get called for interview take your copy of the application form and a copy of your CV so you can refer to them if needed.

54. When not to take 'no' for an answer

When you make an application to a company, whether this is in reply to a specific job or not, you must assume that you are a valid candidate for employment with them. If you have done your research well, you should be able to identify where your unique strengths and abilities will give you a competitive advantage against other candidates. You must believe in yourself and be willing to follow through on your application.

If you have not had a response to your application after a week, you should pick up the phone and speak to the hiring manager. In a polite manner, ask about the status of your application, state why you feel you are *the* compelling candidate and ask if there is any further information required to persuade the hirer to invite you for interview. The secret in making an effective call is to keep it short, polite and think through clearly why they should meet you and make your point.

Not everyone will be comfortable selling themselves in such a direct manner and if you feel you cannot muster the courage to call then consider a follow-up email stating your interest and reasons why you are the candidate they are after.

For some roles and for some people, extreme follow-up techniques may pay dividends. For sales roles particularly, one of the key characteristics most companies look for is tenacity and motivation. Being tenacious (in a polite way) can be a great way to secure a job. Sometimes it is even worth trying to reverse a decision where your application is rejected. The best way to do this is to have a clear understanding of why you are a good candidate for the role and politely but firmly communicate to the hiring manager that you disagree with their decision, state one or two compelling reasons why and ask for an interview. You have nothing to lose at this stage and such an approach can impress some hiring managers. You must however be sure that you are a good candidate and that you are firm but polite in your handling of the situation. You cannot disagree with every rejection or fight every battle but if you have done good preparation in advance then you will know which roles are worth fighting for.

If you believe you are a strong candidate do not be frightened to sell, persuade and fight until you have got the job offer.

Interview well

'Better to remain silent and be thought a fool than to speak out and remove all doubt'
Abraham Lincoln

If you get that all important interview make sure you maximise your chances by following these top tips. If you add up all the effort you put into getting the interview and then add in all the effort that went into job applications that didn't get an interview you will see that it amounts to a lot of hours invested. So do not reduce your chances by just turning up for an interview unprepared and hoping for the best. Luckily for you most people do just that, so if you take the trouble to prepare you will dramatically increase your chances of getting the job.

Most interviewers are also unprepared for the interview meeting; many will have received little training in how to interview well. Some will have read your CV and letter, but many will have just skim read it.

55. Prepare for the interview

Make sure you take time to prepare for the interview. In particular research the company you are applying to, using the techniques described in the research section, making sure you know what businesses they are in and how they are doing.

As a minimum, visit their website and look at the 'about us' section and you will usually find a short statement of what they do:

For example Shell's website states:

'We are a global group of energy and petrochemicals companies with around 101,000 employees in more than 90 countries and territories. Our innovative approach ensures we are ready to help tackle the challenges of the new energy future.'

Also look at their press or news section and find a positive news item you understand and can comment on very briefly.

Early on when you introduce yourself you can add into the dialogue *'I see from your website that you are a global group of energy and petrochemicals companies with around 101,000 employees in more than 90 countries and territories,'* and *'that at present you are bidding for a major exploration project in Rumania'* or some other positive newsworthy event.

It's amazing how many people don't bother and how impressive this sounds to the interviewer if you do make the effort. It immediately shows that you are interested in the company and that you have the initiative to do some research.

56. Know your CV

Make sure you know your way around your CV and what details are in it and what are not. It looks bad if you refer to your CV but can't find the fact you were looking for or find it's not there in that version of the CV. It's a good idea to take three or four spare copies to the interview. You can keep most in your bag, but if the interviewer has lost theirs or two of them need to share you can give them a spare. If you applied through an agency you might find that the interviewer has been provided with an edited version and you then have the opportunity of providing them with an original.

Be able to summarise your CV without reading it verbatim. If you take all your time to read your CV at them this will demonstrate poor communication skills and take up too much time in the interview. If however, you can summarise your skills and each step in your career and relate it to the job requirements, this will sound much more impressive. The interviewers will ask if they want more detail, most candidates give far too much.

57. Rehearse

Even if you frequently attend interviews, rehearse each interview with a friend or family member. The purpose of the rehearsal is not to impress your friend, but to prepare you. Most interviewers do not ask trick questions or use psychologically testing questions. They want to meet you and find out if you can do the job. The questions they will ask will be straightforward.

Questions like:

Why have you applied for this job?

Tell us about yourself.

Why did you (Do you want to) leave your last job?

What are you looking for in a job?

How do you get on with your colleagues?

What are your greatest strengths?

What are your weaknesses?

Do you have any questions to ask us?

Why do you think we should hire you for this job?

(See the next chapter on answering interview questions for what to say in answer to these questions.)

In rehearsal stick to questions like those above plus any specific questions you think you might get asked that relate to the job and answer them in the form:

Interview well

Feature:

Advantage:

Benefit (to them) see below.

After rehearsing a few times you will find that your answers become better and more succinct. This will give you confidence in the interview. You will sound more assured and capable and you are less likely to be stuck for answers. Of course, they may well ask you other questions, but preparing the basics will give you a great start.

In the rehearsal also practise the moment of entering the room, using an 'ice-breaker' to get the conversation going and introducing yourself, see below.

'Hello, great to meet you. I have heard a lot about your firm and I am really looking forward to finding out more.'

'Good morning. I must first thank you for the excellent directions and background information you sent me before this interview.'

'Hello, I was doing some background research prior to coming to this interview and I never realised that...' (use a hook)

58. Dress the part

Make sure that you dress well for the interview. If in doubt both men and women should wear a sober business suit. Do not be tempted by the flashy power tie or up-to-the-minute fashion. Remember they are not interested in your clothes, but what your clothes tell them about your attitude to the job. 'Couldn't be bothered so just put on the first thing to hand' is not a strong selling statement.

You might find that the interviewers are casually dressed without a jacket and tie and might even be wearing jeans. If you are dressed in a suit this is not a problem. It demonstrates respect and that you want the job.

Make sure that if you are wearing a shirt or blouse that it is well ironed. It can often happen that in a warm office you are invited to remove your jacket. A horribly creased 'non-iron' shirt looks bad.

There may be some exceptions, for example, if you are going for the job as a buyer at a fashion house, but unless you have been specifically told otherwise, dress to impress.

Take care also of your personal hygiene, if you didn't shower that morning or are sweating from rushing to the interview it will not help you or the interviewer.

59. Be early

Be early, not on time but at least 15 minutes early, more if your journey is long or complicated. If nearly everything goes wrong, you will still be there before the allotted time. This is incredibly obvious but so often ignored that it is worth emphasising here. Remember if you are early you can wait and be on time. There is absolutely no disadvantage in being early. If you are late there is nothing you can do and in most job interviews it is one of the cardinal sins. Not fatal but hard to recover from. Why is that? First, most jobs involve working with other people or doing work on which others depend. If you or your work is late it has a chain reaction on everyone else. An interview is a time when potential employers try to judge if you can do the job, by turning up late you are demonstrating that you cannot do the simplest part of the job. Not only is it insulting, you are also saying to your employer that you must wait for me. It reveals poor planning skills which are part of any job, if you cannot plan to be there on time, what can you do?

Finally, it is bad for you to be late. If you are late you will be flustered, not in complete control and will add to any normal nervousness you may feel on the day. Also it means that you will start the meeting on a negative, an apology. So being late is a bad thing.

Of course all sorts of events happen that are not your fault to make you late. That is why you plan not to be on time, but to be early. When you arrive you should get as close to where the interview will be or at least check that you are in the right place with a receptionist or secretary. A candidate we know turned up at a large office to a meeting with a marketing manager. The address was correct, but the manager was based in a different building some distance away. If you are early you can compensate not just for your own mistakes, but for those of others too.

If you follow this advice you will get to your interview much too early most of the time. That is good. Do not hide, go to the meeting place and make sure someone knows you are there. You might then be able to go a short distance for a tea or coffee and relax. You will be able to start your interview with a strong positive: 'I was a bit early, but this job is important to me and I wanted to make sure I was on time.'

If, despite all your planning you are still going to be late because of some travel problems, always ring ahead and let people know you will be late and why this has happened. This simple action will go a long way to minimising the problem.

60. Treat the interview as a sales call

In theory interviews are joint discussions where both the candidate and the interviewer have a common goal of determining if the candidate can do the job. In practice the two sides have different agendas. For the candidate it is a sales call where you are the salesperson trying to sell yourself.

Therefore you want to follow the standard sales meeting format:

- A. Prepare
- B. Open
- C. Survey by asking questions
- D. Summarise and check understanding
- E. Demonstrate your ability to do the job
- F. Close

We have already covered preparation. Next we cover each of the other stages and show how they apply in interview. But as well as following the stages of a sales call, you have to think like a salesperson, your job is to enthusiastically sell yourself. In the interview you must demonstrate clearly that you want the job and that you are the best person for it. If you decide later on that this is not the job for you, there will be plenty of time to withdraw.

A sales call never runs over, so check you know how much time you have in the interview and make sure you keep to schedule.

In an interview, the interviewer is in charge and it is important not to challenge his or her authority. However, you don't need to, as the two perspectives of interviewer and candidate fit well together. You must ensure that you cover each of the stages to your satisfaction. If you do the interviewer will also feel that he or she has got what they need and that you have been a willing and enthusiastic partner.

61. Make an entrance – the opening

The first minute or so of an interview is important. People naturally form initial impressions, even if they are aware of this and try not to. The fact that you arrived early and are well dressed will already count in your favour. Most encounters start with a brief 'ice-breaker' comment. Yours can be 'This building was easier to find than I thought, I was eager to be on time, but I ended getting here rather early'. To add to this positive impression you need an opening to introduce yourself. It should be of the form:

Introduction, company flattery, personal claim, outcome desired:

'Good Morning, my name is Mary Smith, I am pleased to be at XYZ company, which has a reputation as the best restaurant in the area, I have over 10 years experience in haute cuisine and I really want to work in a business with a reputation as good as yours.'

You say this in a slow, calm but purposeful voice. You can do this because you've practised it. The introduction is very short and then you STOP TALKING. It is their meeting and they will introduce themselves.

By now your smart dress, punctuality and calm but authoritative introduction will have put you in the top 10% of candidates.

62. Survey the job and the key requirements

The interviewer should start by describing what the job entails, but they may think that this information has already been provided and jump straight in with a question about your CV.

This allows you to counter with:

'OK, but can I first make sure I fully understand what you are looking for, so that I can explain my CV in the most helpful way.'

Be careful of course, not to sound as if you are taking over the interview.

So either the interviewer has explained the job, or you have got him or her to explain it. In the conversation make sure you understand all the job criteria, that is all the features or qualities that the interviewer is looking for. You do this by asking simple questions like:

What skills and knowledge are most important?

What personal qualities does the successful candidate need?

You now summarise the key points back to the interviewer listing the key requirements of the job and what benefits they bring to the employer. There are likely to be a short list of these. One example might be:

'You are looking for a manager with at least five years experience so that they can immediately contribute without being closely supervised.'

If you do a good summary of the job and the requirements, it will sound to the interviewer that you have been listening and

Interview well

that you really understand. That is flattering to the interviewer, plus the ability to listen to others and learn is important in all jobs, so you win on two fronts and you are now sure you know what is important.

63. Demonstrate that you can do the job

Once you have finished the discussion of the job and its requirements it is time to move onto the part where you show you have all the right qualities. The fact that you have just summarised them means you can keep your description of your own experience focussed on those things that are relevant and explain how you can deliver benefits to the company. If the interviewer doesn't suggest this after the summary, you can do it yourself by saying something like:

'Would it be helpful if I told you something about my experience?'

Most people have led interesting lives full of unique experiences, but listening to it can be boring. It's like looking at collections of vacation photos. Unless you were on the vacation, it gets boring after the first few pictures.

So when it's your turn to talk about yourself, don't go through every detail of your CV in minute detail. Only talk about those things that are relevant.

To do this talk in FAB mode: Feature, Advantage and Benefit when describing your own experience.

Feature is a fact about you

Advantage says what this means

Benefit is the 'So what' to the hiring company

For example if you were applying for a job as a project manager in a software development firm:

Interview well

Feature: I have led teams of ten or more people to deliver projects.

Advantage: I can lead and manage people to get things done on time.

Benefit: All the projects I lead for you will be on time.

Any feature or fact about you that does not deliver a benefit to the company is irrelevant for the purposes of the interview.

64. Close and follow up

After you have talked about yourself with the interviewer, the interview will wind down. Most interviewers will signal the end by saying something like: 'Is there anything else you would like to ask?' If you have some real questions ask them here. Often you will not have, in which case you should ask:

'I am really enthusiastic about this job, have I given you enough information to make a decision?'

You are unlikely to get a straight answer, but the interviewer might use this as an opportunity to revisit something they did not quite understand. At a minimum it demonstrates that you really do want the job.

Then say:

'I am really keen to progress further in this process. What happens next?' So that you are clear about what the next step is and when you will hear.

The same day write a short letter or email to the interviewer thanking him for the opportunity to interview and re-affirming your commitment.

Organisations will often hire a less qualified candidate who really wants the job over one who is well qualified but less committed.

Ten interview questions you must be able to answer

'No question is so difficult to answer as that to which the answer is obvious'
George Bernard Shaw

At some point in the selection process you will have to meet the person who is hiring you so that they can decide if you are a good fit to the job. Most interviewers have not been trained in advanced interview techniques or human psychology so will ask straightforward questions to try and understand what you have to offer.

As described in earlier sections you will already have done some research or asked your own questions so that you know what the job is for, what benefits it brings to the organisation. One way to understand this is to ask yourself, 'What good things, from a company point of view, happen as a result of someone doing this job well?' This is the benefit to the organisation; you must understand this benefit so that you can answer questions well.

For example, a receptionist is not just there to answer the phone; he or she is there to create a strong positive impression with visitors by greeting them warmly and dealing with them efficiently; they are the public face and main ambassadors for the organisation. Similarly a project manager is there to get projects completed on time and budget thus contributing to the organisation's profits. A warehouse worker ensures the efficient and timely dispatch of goods thus increasing customer loyalty.

Make sure that you answer questions using the Feature-Advantage-Benefit method described earlier. Where:

Feature: is something you have: five years experience greeting people for a top organisation; a Prince2 project management qualification, or the ability to lift heavy weights.

Advantage: is what you can do as a result: understand the importance of first impressions, run a project in a structured way, retrieve any item no matter how big.

Benefit: is how it helps the organisation meet its aims: let visitors know they are valued, ensure projects are delivered profitably, and keep customers' delivery promises.

In simpler terms imagine that after every answer you give the recruiter is asking: 'What's in it for me (or my organisation)?'

Below are ten questions you must be able to answer. They will crop up in most interviews sometimes in a slightly different form. Therefore make sure you rehearse answering them. Use a friend or family member to ask the questions. By rehearsing you will find you give better more concise answers and allow yourself time to think in the interview.

Rehearsal will also allow you to practise how you answer the questions. Your answers must be delivered in an enthusiastic style that shows that you really want the job (even if you are unsure). The authors have seen enthusiastic, cheerful people get jobs ahead of better qualified candidates who answer questions in a long-winded and flat manner. They probably did that because they were nervous and just said what came into their head and kept on talking or worse still, answered with

Ten interview questions you must be able to answer

short answers of a couple of words. If you practise answering these questions you won't do that.

The ten questions:

65. Why have you applied for this job?

You answer this by thinking of the objectives of the department you are joining and relating it to that.

So our receptionist might say:

'Every person I have met from XYZ company is interested in me and what I want, they really listen. I want to join a company like that.'

Followed by a relevant FAB statement:

'I am looking for a job that will use my people skills and that I will enjoy **(Feature)**. *I will bring enthusiasm to the job of receptionist* **(Advantage)** *and I can assure you that everyone I meet or talk to on the telephone will leave with a positive impression of the company* **(Benefit**).*'*

Of course the real reason you have applied is because it meets a need of yours, but that is unlikely to be relevant to the employer. So you might have joined because it's close to home, a friend works there; it pays well; or you just want a job and this one will do.

You might mention some of these reasons if they also help the organisation, for example:

'I live close by **(Feature)** *so I will always be on time* **(Advantage)** *ensuring that visitors are always met* **(Benefit)**.*'*

66. Tell us about yourself

In our experience most candidates take this as an opportunity to bore the interviewer silly for at least 30 minutes by reading their CV out loud and adding lots of extra detail. As an interviewer that's not why they asked, they were looking for two things, first for the job seeker to highlight their main strengths that are relevant to the job and second to see how well they communicate. This is a helpful question and gives you the ability to run through your CV in a way that you control. The trick here is not to take too long. After about ten minutes the recruiter will lose concentration and they will not be listening. So you should practise going through your CV without reading it and highlighting each position that illustrates a point you wish to make, what you have achieved (Feature), what this allows you to do (Advantage) and how that will be of benefit to the organisation you want to join.

You start and end this description with your summary of personal strengths. If you do this well you can hit the interview version of a 'Home Run' by demonstrating understanding of the job, your own qualifications and good communication skills.

67. Why did you (Do you want to) leave your last job?

You should answer this question in a way that suggests that this job is the one you have been searching for, it is great, it is your dream job. You can always change your mind later if you get a better offer.

The answer to this question should be framed so that it makes sense to the employer and gives them an employee who wants to do the job and who is qualified to do it. This applies even if you are unemployed. If you are unemployed you may be doing some voluntary work (see earlier section) and can relate the answer to that.

The reason you left could be that you were made redundant; this doesn't mean that your new employer assumes you will accept any role. The job should reflect your natural progression in life.

If you are in a job it should be easier as you can relate the new opportunity to the old one.

In all cases the reason needs to be a positive progression that benefits the employer.

The golden rule is: never insult or heavily criticise an old employer, even if the old employer had many faults. It will sound as though you are making excuses for yourself and avoiding taking responsibility for your own actions. What you can do is place a shortcoming among some positives, this gives the impression of a balanced view, but allows you a reason for leaving.

Ten interview questions you must be able to answer

So for any category of job seeker it gives you the space to at least say something like:

'My last employer struggled in the market, the company had good products and many good people but was lacking in marketing expertise. I am looking for a solid all-round organisation with an outstanding reputation like yours that I can contribute to and learn from.'

Alternatively there may be something real that you need from a job that benefits the employer, particularly if you have experience and you are looking for a bigger job.

That would be an answer like:

'At my last company I gained a lot of experience and have (FAB statement here) now I am looking for more responsibility and in particular to lead my own projects. I have solid experience as a deputy project manager and a proven track record that will allow me to deliver projects on time for you.'

68. What are you looking for in a job?

In general you should already have described how this role is a natural follow-on from your previous job. It allows you to build on the skills and experience you already have, but also provides new challenges. This gives you the scope to describe those skills and knowledge and show how they benefit the company.

When answering this question you also reflect back the key requirements of the job as your personal goals. If the job requires leading a team of people then your answer should include that you really enjoy working in teams and in particular helping both the team and individuals achieve the goal that has been set.

Similarly if you are applying for a job as a night security guard, what you are looking for might be to work for a recognised company or to be able to make a contribution to the security of the company. As this job might require working alone, you might say that you are also looking for the chance to demonstrate your personal autonomy and senses of authority.

It is important that the answer is credible and that you do not ignore any obvious challenges of the job, but acknowledge them as part of a bigger attraction. In the case of our security guard, some might consider working nights, alone a drawback. You can turn this into a positive by saying that although some might consider it a disadvantage you see it as the other side of a job that gives the autonomy you seek.

A job as a consultant might require lengthy stays away from home, the advantage to you might be the ability to completely immerse yourself in a customer project free from distractions.

Ten interview questions you must be able to answer

Beware of leading with reasons that are benefits to you but not to the employer. If one of the advantages is that you can earn more money then you need to link that to an employer-related benefit reason. The most common way is to say that you welcome the challenge of contributing to the organisation and the fact that the pay reflects your contribution.

69. How do you get on with your colleagues?

Before answering this question think through the personal relationships required to do this job. There will be several dimensions to this. There will be the managers you work for, those you work with and often those who work for you. In addition there will often be people who are not in your chain of command that you need to work with and perhaps influence indirectly, such as people in another department.

Draw a simple diagram of these associations and then think about the different type of relationships you need with each and which ones are the most important for this job.

So, for example, if you are going to spend most of your time in a large team of people then you need to emphasise your collaborative relationships. If you were going to work as a leader then you might focus on your ability to give clear direction yet still be consultative.

In many jobs you need a mixture, but for your particular job choose the two or three types that are most important and then use the FAB formula to point to your experience (Feature) and relate it to how you can be in your new job (Advantage) and how that will help get the work done (Benefit).

70. What are your greatest strengths?

From your Personal Profile you should already know your core strengths and why they are important. This is an opportunity to restate them and draw upon your CV to emphasise them and relate them to the job requirements (FAB) again. Keep this answer short; a long answer can demonstrate that one of your weaknesses is poor communication skills.

This is a more dangerous formulation of the question: 'What achievements are you most proud of?' You may have a personal achievement of which you are justifiably proud. For example you may hold the world record for the consumption of oysters or you may have survived a nasty personal crisis. These are unlikely to help get the job even though they may be impressive. It is tempting to talk about things which you may be justifiably proud of. Before you do, ask yourself, how does the quality displayed help the hiring organisation?

Choose two or three relevant achievements that demonstrate key strengths. A salesperson might be proud of being the only person to hit their numbers six quarters in a row; a manager will be proud of coaching individuals to win promotions. A project manager will be proud of a particular project that they steered through adversity to deliver on time.

71. What are your weaknesses?

This is a tricky question; you need to talk about genuine weaknesses, but in a way that shows you have learned from them and that this learning will help with the job.

The first and the best way, is to talk about your need to improve a skill in which you are already strong. For example if you already speak English and French well, you might talk about your Spanish as weakness you want to improve.

Chefs might talk about improving their ability to cook Asian food and software engineers might talk about learning a particular new technology.

In each case the weakness you are describing is against a background of relative strength in the area and demonstrates self awareness and a commitment to learning.

The second way is to think of the most important qualities required for the job and then to confess your relative intolerance for the opposite.

A customer care call centre person may need good listening skills and patience. Your weakness might be that sometimes you seem too sympathetic to people in difficulty and you have become a magnet for colleagues who often confide in you.

A project manager might talk about their intolerance of chaos and how every time they see a problem they want to jump in and sort it out.

Ten interview questions you must be able to answer

A good general purpose weakness is to be annoyed by people who are routinely late. You can say that this annoys you as it can waste everyone's time and is disrespectful to others.

Make sure of course that the weakness is credible and really is part of your character; if you were late for the interview the last weakness may not work, although you can say that it caused you to be annoyed with yourself.

This question is a particularly important one to practise. Often when candidates are asked, they seem surprised and have to think long and hard before answering, which gives the impression that they are hunting for a credible lie. Answering too quickly a question about a weakness makes it look like you are over-proud of it.

The right way is a slight pause, which gives the impression that you are being honest about something you might not otherwise have said.

72. Do you have any hobbies or play any sports?

This question is likely to come up after the interviewer has finished going through your CV. Remember that you are being interviewed for a job, not as friend or sports expert, unless of course you are applying to be a television pundit.

Interviewers ask this question for one of two reasons: they have heard other people ask it or they have run out of other questions or they hope it will reveal a side of your personality that has remained hidden. Do not get carried away in a lengthy description of something you may be interested in, but is not relevant to the job.

This question needs to be answered briefly, but in a way that supports the picture of yourself that you have painted. It can provide additional evidence for some aspects of your character that you want to emphasise, like responsibility or teamwork. Beware that it can also reveal things that might make you less attractive to your employer. As with every other answer to a question, you need to be asking yourself, how will this benefit my employer?

If you participate in team sports or you have a position of responsibility this is evidence of qualities that might be useful to your employer. You can give information in the FAB format to underline this. For example If you are captain of the local football club, and you are applying for a job that involves managing a group, you can talk about how your football experience has helped you understand how to motivate people

Ten interview questions you must be able to answer

and get the best out of them; and how you take this position seriously.

Beware of answers that may ring alarm bells in the interviewer. If you show a real passion for an activity and it is clear that the activity is very time consuming, then although you may see it as dedication to a cause and evidence of what you can achieve, your employer may see it as a distraction. They may view you as a clock watcher who will disappear at exactly 5pm to go training, or someone who needs time off to participate in competitions or uses work time to organise personal events.

If you are a weekend golfer that is fine, if you are a competitive low-handicap player, when do you get time to practise? If you climb mountains, will you need time off to go on overseas expeditions and spend work time on logistics planning.

Remember that a reasonable range of pastimes demonstrates a balanced life and can be used to highlight qualities of value to an employer that will help your application. Time consuming or distracting interests could prove a liability. Do not spend too much time answering this question.

73. Do you have any questions to ask us?

It may seem odd to say, but make sure you use this question to ask about anything you are genuinely unclear about, for example the pay and conditions, duties and so forth. Make sure that you have read any letters or documentation carefully so you don't ask about something they have already told you, but do ask if the information is unclear.

However do not ask questions about trivia, such as *'Do I get a reserved parking space?'* or *'What is the food like in the company canteen?'*

Relevant questions that are clearly important to you such as pay are interpreted as 'buying signals' by the interviewer; they show that you are really interested in the job. If pay has not been mentioned and you don't ask this will seem strange.

After you have had your questions answered you can summarise why you are a good fit and end with:

'I am really enthusiastic about this job, have I given you enough information to make a decision?'

Then ask: *'What happens next?'* so you are clear about what the next step is and when you will hear.

Ten interview questions you must be able to answer

74. Why do you think we should hire you for this job?

This is a useful question to get; it lets you finish on a high by demonstrating that you understand the requirements of the job; showing that you meet the requirements, checking that you have not missed anything and most importantly showing and saying that you really want the job.

The first step in this is to summarise back to them the key requirements of the job. There should be no more than three to five points and the reasons they are important. A software engineer might say:

'From what you have said, my understanding of the requirements are:
A strong knowledge of C and structured programming.
The ability to write good documentation to reduce the cost of maintenance.
Good interpersonal skills to fit into the team.
Proven ability to deliver on time so that software is delivered to customer deadlines.'

After this step you check: 'Are these the major requirements?'

This proves to your interviewer that you were listening and understood and he or she will feel that you are taking responsibility and communicating well. If the summary is corrected you restate it and get agreement.

You now have the perfect platform to summarise back to your interviewer how you meet each of these key requirements. Earlier in the interview you will have already explained these in depth, so it is important that you keep your reminders brief. Our software engineer might start by saying:

'As we have discussed I am confident that I can meet all of these requirements:

I have used C directly in my last three major projects and was the C expert on project Y **(Feature)**. I have an in-depth knowledge of the language **(Advantage)** which means I can be productive from day one **(Benefit)**...'

You then finish with a restatement of your enthusiasm for the job and a question that lets them know you are already thinking of starting.

'As you can see I have the skills you are looking for and I really want to work at XYZ company. When do you think I will know if I have been successful?'

You will get other questions, but these ten seem to recur and represent a good foundation for you to build your interview upon. You will probably get specific questions about your line of work; if you know what they are add them to your list. However, the questions above represent the core of what interviewers are trying to find out.

All questions should be answered with enthusiasm and in a lively manner.

None of these questions should come as a surprise. Therefore you should practise answering them before each job interview as the answers will be different depending on the organisation and also perhaps on whom you are meeting. If you practise you will surprise yourself and stun your potential employer by delivering concise and well-thought-out answers in a confident

Ten interview questions you must be able to answer

manner. You will also reduce any nervousness or anxiety you have because you will be confident that you can answer most questions that come up.

Questions interviewees should ask

'A wise man can learn more from a foolish question than a fool can learn from a wise answer'
Bruce Lee

Asking questions helps you to sell yourself to an employer. It gives you the opportunity to demonstrate interest, show you have researched the employer and that you take them seriously. Questions can be split into job specific such as 'where will I be based?', 'who does the role report to?' and more expansive questions that look at the company and its culture, business dynamics etc.

You can have a prepared list of questions that can be recycled for most interviews but other questions need to be researched in advance and used intelligently during the interview.

Some of these questions might occur as part of the natural flow of the interview, but they can also be used to open up the interview and create more of a discussion.

One of the important areas you should ask about is pay and conditions. This is so important it gets its own section following this one. In this section we will give advice on more general questioning technique and some specific questions you may want to ask.

- Questions interviewees should ask

75. Learn effective questioning techniques

In an interview you must allow the interviewer to run the interview and conform to their structure, pace and format. Do not start firing questions straight from the start of the interview or disrupt the flow of the interview through questioning. The early part of the interview will be about the job; your skills and experience. In this phase follow the interviewers lead and only ask question of clarification.

There will be a natural time near the end where you can ask questions or will be invited to do so. It is good practice to check how much time you have to ask questions and to stay within these limits. Many candidates have failed because the interviewee has spoken for too long, asked hundreds of questions and become irritating.

Always start with bigger and more generalised open questions and leave detailed questions for the end. Listen to the answers and demonstrate that you are paying attention and be prepared and equipped to take notes.

Asking questions enables you to understand if the role is right for you and also to gain an insight into particular things the hirer is looking for; therefore helping you to be effective in subsequent interviews. Questioning also allows you to demonstrate that you have researched the employer and have a real interest in working there.

76. What will the first 100 days look like?

This question can give you a good insight into the role and its initial challenges. It also gives you some strong material to match your skills and experience against their requirements.

It is possible that if you ask this question it may be turned back to you where the interviewer will ask you *'well, what would you expect to do or achieve in the first 100 days?'* You must be prepared for this and prepare for it in advance. In order not to seem arrogant you should preface any answer by stating that you do not have complete information and your first actions in the role would be getting to know how things are, how things get done and what the real issues and challenges are but on the information you currently have you would suggest...

Then answer covering some or all of these topics:

Understanding the objectives of the job
Meeting the key players: colleagues, customers etc.
Listening
Formulating a plan and getting agreement
Getting a quick win and proving yourself
Staying focussed on the main requirements of the job

77. What are your key selection criteria?

You should have covered this in the 'Survey' part of the interview described in the earlier chapter. However, if you didn't get the chance you can ask it towards the end of the interview. Usually you will have an advertisement or job specification detailing the skills required for the role. Asking this question may seem superfluous, but in fact you will gain some useful insight into the prioritisation of skills and background required to be the successful candidate – information that you will use to your benefit at later stages of the selection process.

It is perfectly valid to ask the interviewer what they are looking for in a successful candidate. It enables you to understand if you are a strong candidate or if you are wasting your time. It also enables you to understand what they need to find out, thereby assisting you in refining your messages and sales pitch.

78. Why did you invite me for interview?

This question needs to be addressed at interview and ideally early in the process. A good way to ask this is 'what was it in my background that particularly swayed your decision to invite me for interview?'

The answer to this question may give you useful information on how an interviewer views you from your CV and what your competitive advantages may be. You can use this information to compare yourself against the criteria they have stated.

Questions interviewees should ask

79. What are the biggest challenges facing your company?

The answer provides additional insight allowing you to answer questions with information that is focussed on areas that are of particular concern to them. Hiring managers are human beings (it's true) and like to talk about what interests and affects them. This question can generally get them into their comfort zone speaking about their job, their company and their challenges. It can be a great opportunity to get some good insights and engage in a collaborative discussion of what the challenges are and how you could help address them.

When you talk about how you might address challenges facing the company, there is a danger that you will offer a suggestion they have tried and failed at, or suggest that they have missed something. To avoid this always make suggestions in the third person, that is talk about how other successful companies have tackled the problem. Then if they reject your suggestion they are not rejecting you or being defensive. For example:

'Many companies I have worked with have found that one of the best ways of increasing productivity is to establish formal schemes to gather and reward suggestions from staff.'

80. Have I answered your question fully?

This is a question that you should use throughout the interview process.

Getting the right amount of detail in an answer is critical to a successful interview. Some interviewers want limited information from you on some subjects and more on others. It can be a challenge to get the right level of detail on every answer. A common mistake is to give too much detail; candidates get onto a roll and will not stop talking.

This is one of the commonest reasons for failing at interview.

Too little detail on answers can also prove fatal. The best strategy is to be concise but answer each question directly and ideally using a real example from your past experiences. Use your judgement on how much detail to give on each answer but frequently validate this by asking a variation on 'have I given you enough detail?'

81. What is the selection process?

This question should be asked as early in the selection process as possible. Ideally you should ask this question even before attending the first interview. What you need to find out is how many interviews there are, who they will be with, what are the interviewers looking for, will you be expected to do any special preparation, will you need to take any tests etc.

Knowledge of these issues enables you to plan and prepare in advance. It is easy to lose an opportunity by attending an interview that may take an unexpected turn and this can undermine confidence and seriously degrade your performance.

82. What are the good things and what are the challenges about working for this company

This is a good open ended question (actually two questions) that can get the interviewer really engaged in answering. How they answer can be very useful in deciding if the role is right for you. The way this question is answered will give you a great insight into the employer; more positives than negatives can be a good indicator for the culture of the organisation whereas an overly negative response may indicate poor morale.

This type of question is useful for opening up a two-way dialogue with the interviewer especially if you ask subsequent questions to elaborate on some of the information given in the answers. Be aware that you need to retain a positive manner even through the 'bad bits of the company' answers as too much dwelling on the negative may reflect badly on you.

Questions interviewees should ask

83. When can I start?

Yes this is bold, but it does demonstrate enthusiasm, interest and commitment, attributes that most employers are looking for. It fits naturally into the closing phase of the interview described earlier. There are gentle and less direct ways of asking a question like this. You could try variations such as

'I am on two weeks' notice and would be really keen to start as soon as possible. When would you ideally like me to start?'

'This is the best and most exciting role I have interviewed for so far – I want to join – is there anything else you need to know from me before you can make me an offer?'

When you are looking for a job, whether you are comfortable with it or not, you must be a salesperson. Salespeople need to sell and a key part of selling is closing, that is asking for a decision. Many candidates fall at the final hurdle because they fail to demonstrate sufficient desire for the role. It is not that they lack desire, it is only that they have failed to demonstrate and communicate this. A closing question is a great way to demonstrate a high level of interest. Be brave, you may only get one chance!

Manage the recruitment process

'The meek will inherit the earth, as long as it's okay by everyone else' Anon

Finding and getting a job is a process, you need to understand how recruiters and companies go about it, what the stages are and how you can influence the process to your advantage. How you are treated by the process depends on how you behave. You can either be a passive victim waiting for things to happen or you can be an active driver and make things happen. Needless to say, the more active approach is more likely to get results. If in doubt take control. The only things that come to those who wait are buses, everything else you must go and get. Waiting is what you do while other people are getting jobs.

84. Discover the process

Even at the application stage for a job, you can ask: 'What happens now?' Whether it is a direct recruitment or through an agency there will be an answer even if it's incomplete. You need to ask the question so you can discover the process and make it work to your advantage. It's a very reasonable question and demonstrates your interest.

If you are applying through an agency or recruitment company, then they will have been asked to submit a number of candidates by a date to a manager in the recruiting organisation. At the very least find out the date and let the recruiter know (politely) that you will be checking in with him or her just before that time. Then do just that, phone and ask if you have been put forward; how many other candidates there are; what happens after this initial submission, when will the initial interviews be and with who. Find out when they need someone by and as many of the steps in the process you can. Let the recruiter know in a friendly way that you are enthusiastic about the opportunity. Grabbing the process like this will dramatically increase your chances of being put forward to the employer because the recruiter wants people who are genuinely enthusiastic, plus if the recruiter has any doubts, you get the chance to explain why you should be chosen over someone else.

The employing company will have a similar process. In most large companies it will be necessary to raise a 'Recruiting Requisition' or something similar, which is a form giving the hiring manager authority to hire. That form will list the job requirements, pay and expected start date. If your initial application is through an HR department, it is quite reasonable to phone, to check that they have received your application, that everything is in order and then to ask about the process. Keep asking about dates and people until you sense they don't want to tell you more. Make a friend of this person and later you can call back to ask how the process is going.

Some companies will have tasks they want candidates to do in the process such as preparing presentations, responding to communications, coming back with further information etc. Listen very carefully to what these requirements are and deliver against them perfectly, on time and with no omissions. Though such details can seem unimportant, many companies see compliance as demonstrating commitment, listening and comprehension. Failure to deliver (even in the smallest way) can be a short cut to a rejection.

Even if you are applying to a small business there will be an informal process, find out what is and track it. At all times be polite, don't make unnecessary calls, but do contact before important milestones and selection points.

85. Don't fret about delays

Despite the opening advice, sometimes you must wait, but you are doing so not to be passive, but because you understand the process. Large companies can be bureaucratic so no news usually means just that, nothing has happened. Often in a recruitment process the people who get the fastest feedback will be those who are rejected. This is where knowing the process will help. If you have applied and know the likely date of first interviews, you can just wait until a few days before. If you have still heard nothing you can enquire. Given that you expected to be told by a certain date it is perfectly reasonable to check.

Often there is a delay after rejecting the obvious misfits, the remaining possible longlist candidates may need to be discussed within the organisation and then dates arranged for those who will be doing the interviews. In a busy organisation it can often be difficult to get agreed dates.

Similarly after the shortlist interviews when a final candidate is to be selected, it may need further approval to hire from senior managers, which can also cause delay.

86. Be in the area

If you have been able to find out who the hiring manager is you may be able to short cut the process by being 'in the area'. Using this technique, you create a well-researched reason for having to be close to the organisation. Usually a business meeting of some sort that does not conflict with the organisation you are applying to. You need to make this created opportunity as real as possible. You need a specific organisation and address and a neutral time. Lunch is best as it keeps you free both late morning and early afternoon.

Armed with this created opportunity you contact the hiring manager, by phone or email, saying that you are in the area and would very much like to stop by and take five minutes to introduce yourself either late morning or early afternoon. You may get a brisk rejection, but you may also get accepted and have the opportunity to dramatically increase your chances of selection.

Asking for five minutes makes it more difficult to refuse and makes the meeting more likely. If you get the meeting keep it to five minutes and only stay longer if the time increase is specifically suggested by the person you meet. Show that you can manage time and that your time is as valuable as theirs.

87. Accelerate the process

Your response to all requests from recruiters and employers should be immediate and reliable. If you get back to employers quickly with dates for meetings and return recruiters' phone calls the same day you will develop an impression of reliability and commitment. It is just this sort of quality that employers are usually looking for, by contrast if you delay, or worse still you are late in responding you will move towards the bottom of the pile. You must cultivate an attitude of impatience and a propensity to action.

Be aware of the value of time, both your time and that of your potential employers. You can cut chunks out of their time by quick responses and cut chunks out of your time by managing them and setting an example of urgency. If you are first to return calls, first to answer questions and take the first available interview space, you put yourself at the head of the queue. It will not guarantee success but it will increase your odds. If a recruiter is looking to draw up a shortlist for interview and you get back to them first, you're on the list. If you get back last they may have to remove someone else to give you a place.

88. Show desire

The authors have met hundreds, probably thousands of candidates when filling hundreds of jobs at all levels. The candidates that stand out are the ones that are enthusiastic and committed to getting a job. You know they want the job and they are itching to do whatever it takes to make it happen. There are comparatively few of these people and they are gold dust, the vast majority of candidates are forgettable and passive.

If an interviewee answers questions in a flat uninteresting way, the interviewer turns off; they may not even hear what is said. In an interview round it is common to see six or more people and listen to them describe themselves and why they want the job. If the candidate is passive and boring it is very easy for the interviewer to tune out. Organisations do not want to hire people who cause that sort of reaction. To make an impact, be memorable in your own way, not by being something you are not but by showing in everything that you do or say that you really do want this job.

After groups of interviews it is usual for those interviewing to meet to discuss the candidates. It is common to find that people focus on discussing those people who stood out; often these candidates will be forgiven for not having quite the right skills or experience. To increase your chances you must become one of those people who are remembered.

89. Walk the talk

Recruitment is an imperfect process, through telephone calls, letters and meetings with the candidate employers are trying to assess how each person might perform if they were doing the job on offer. They will need to imagine what that person would be like as a part of their team, or a colleague. You can help them by acting and dressing the part, be the new receptionist, sales manager, director of finance. Practise at home and in the interview try and act as if you already have the job. A senior manager will be calm and authoritative; a receptionist might be bright, chatty and helpful. Anything that you can do to bridge the gap between you as the candidate and you as the job holder will get you closer to the real thing.

In an interview visualise yourself in the role dealing with the interviewer as a colleague, stop playing the eager-to-please candidate and be the enthusiastic businesslike co-worker.

Make sure that you acknowledge all communications, from telephone calls to meetings. If they communicate to you via email, use that, if they write letters do the same. Be businesslike, brief and to the point and re-emphasise your commitment to the job. For example, even after a telephone call you might reply with a brief email or letter saying:

Thanks for your call on Wednesday; it was useful to learn about the delay in the interviews. I remain excited about the prospect of joining Xco and look forward to speaking with you soon.

Do this even for rejection letters, saying that you are disappointed, but hope to hear about other opportunities.

90. Know the decision makers

At the start of this section we said that you must understand the process. It is just as important to know the people in the process. Find out all you can about the individuals and their backgrounds. Some of this was covered in the earlier section on research.

There are three main sources for this:

The first is to ask. Your initial point of contact for a job might be a recruiter, agency, or an administrator or secretary at the actual company. Even if your next step is just a phone call ask your contact 'can you tell me a bit about Mr or Mrs X, what is his or her background'. As long as you ask in a relaxed way, people will give you snippets of useful information. Even in an interview you can ask the question of the interviewer. It sounds flattering and will give you a useful insight into how they might think about you. Interviewers will interpret this question as a genuine interest in other people. In all cases don't go too far, ask one question and a follow-up question and then move on.

The second-best place to get information is on social networking sites. Although Facebook is the most popular, people use it mostly for non-business use and the information you can see there might not be that helpful. Facebook's privacy features will usually mean you can see information only on friends and friends of friends, but it's worth a try. You may discover that you do have a mutual friend that gives you another access point. See below and in the earlier section on sources of jobs. Far better sources are business networking sites such as LinkedIn (www.linkedin.com). On these sites people describe themselves in their professional capacity. The entries look like abbreviated CVs so you see what they have done in the past. You can also find mutual colleagues and possibly organisations where you both worked, even at different times. Because these sites present each person's public business face, they are usually widely accessible, so you can see the basic details without having any direct connection including any special interest groups they belong to. A word of warning, do not initiate a new contact and try to make them a 'friend' during the recruitment process, if they aren't one already. This will be seen as an unwarranted intrusion.

The third source of information is to ask friends and colleagues if they know this person. At least some of your job contacts should be coming through personal contacts, so don't forget to use them to the full and get a briefing. Even if your job came from other means it might be worth a quick email to selected friends seeing if they know anyone from the company you are applying to.

One you have this information, use it wisely. Do not assume it is correct, some of your sources might be well meaning but inaccurate, but do use it to highlight aspects of your background where there might be mutual interest. For example if your potential manager used to be an accountant you might talk about your ability to understand the basics of company accounts. If you hit a real area of interest it will prompt further questioning. Use information that identifies areas of commonality with people in the organisation. The more you can show you are like them, the more they will like you and people hire people they like.

91. Match responses to the stage and the person

When you have any communication about a job, think about why they are asking or what they are saying. Think about the person who is communicating; what their role is in the recruitment process and what decision or action they need to make from the communication they are now making.

Avoid giving too much or the wrong information to the person asking and waste their time. Listen carefully to what is asked, think about the purpose of the question, pause to think, and give an appropriate answer, followed if necessary by a message, in FAB form about you. (FAB mode: Feature, Advantage and Benefit when describing your own experience: Feature is a fact about you; Advantage says what this means; Benefit is the 'So what' to the hiring company.)

This applies not just in interviews but in all communications. If you get a call from an administrator to book an interview time, first answer the question, then say how great it is to hear from the company, enquire about the process and then stop talking. You will appear confident, committed and businesslike. If you waffle on about yourself, you may be wasting their time and creating the impression of a woolly thinker.

The authors have had the painful experience of telling a candidate that the interview was an hour, giving a brief outline of the job, and then being bored to tears as the candidate spent the remaining 50 minutes going through their CV in minute detail, even adding new bits of information. The candidate had demonstrated that they didn't listen, couldn't communicate, had little interest in the job or the person in front of them and left having learned nothing.

Manage the recruitment process

In a first interview you talk about your CV at a high level, going through it quickly but efficiently. Your main aim is to provide an outline of yourself, but more importantly to get into a dialogue so that you can build a connection with the person and they can gain experience of you as a future employee. You need to give them enough data about you to answer the question, but also show your interest in the job and your ability to engage with them.

Subsequent meetings, calls and emails are dealt with similarly, listen to what is said, pause to think, then answer the question and slip in a benefit about yourself.

92. Manage references

References come in many forms. The most common are either formal reference letters that are addressed to a general audience and are from someone in authority, or individual references taken after a job offer.

A pre-written or formal reference serves a similar purpose to an educational certificate. They are from an appropriate authority and they certify that you can do something.

For example if you are going for a job as a security guard, then such a letter from a head of security or a trusted public figure such as a company finance director is appropriate. In education you might get a letter from a head of school. In general, pre-written references are most effective where the person is hard to get hold of and could not be expected to respond in a timely manner to individual requests, and where by giving a general reference, the person in authority is putting their reputation on the line. They will be brief and verifiable, so it should be possible for a company to phone an administrator at the office of this person to check its authenticity, or at least that you are known.

To be worth using, these references need to come from a person in authority, the higher the better, and to be on headed paper. There is no point In having a general reference from a friend or ordinary colleague.

The advantage of these references is that you can see exactly what is written and you can supply the reference instantly. If you can get references from a suitably high authority, they are very valuable and can boost your reputation and chances of

Manage the recruitment process

getting the job. In certain professions, like teaching, they are common, but strangely they are rare in general commerce, so use them if you can, to get an advantage.

Individual references taken after a job offer, are more common. However these are normally taken up after a job offer has been made as a final insurance against any skeletons in the closet or untruths in the CV. As such, although they are important they cannot help boost your chances, they can only stop you getting a job you are being offered. The most common difficulty is that referees are hard to get hold of or slow to respond. It's your job to manage them.

First, when you start your job application campaign for multiple jobs, you need to try and get at least five referees, ideally three people you have worked for and two you have worked with. You need multiple bosses in order to choose the right one to match the job and also to have spare capacity in case one is away when you need them, or you have to ask for references for multiple jobs and may not want to overburden them. You need to contact all of these in advance and check they are willing to act as referees, but tell them that this will only be required once you are about to be offered a job.

Make sure you have their correct details, including: current job title and organisation, business address, telephone numbers and email address. Don't just use the details you have, check that these are the contact details you can use for reference purposes. Warn them that these references may be written or they may get a phone call.

Check the application process, but unless specified, it is common practice to put 'References upon Request' on your CV.

This gives you control and ensures you know when referees are to be contacted.

When the recruiting organisation says they want to take up references, ask by what means they will be doing so: verbal or written, and then say you will alert your referees.

You should then check with your referees that they are available and willing and then send them a note so that they know what to put. You don't write the reference for them but usually send them an email specifying precisely the job, you are going for, who will call and most importantly four or five key FAB statements you want them to cover that match the main demands of the job:

For example:

-Skilled in C++ and able to mentor others
-Gifted software engineer who delivers on time
-Punctual and careful in their work, so can be relied upon
-Sociable and a strong team player
-Has led groups of six or more developers and has good people-management skills

You then go back to the recruiting organisation with the details, ask when they will contact the referees and ask when they expect replies by. You then manage that process by reminding your referees and checking for receipt of references with the organisation.

Manage the recruitment process

93. Treat everyone as important

It is easy to be on your best behaviour when dealing with the hiring manager or a senior executive, but most recruitment processes will involve people from across the organisation, be nice to them too, here's why.

In the interview process many organisations involve a wide selection of people to judge whether you will be a good fit to the team. So you may get to meet a group of potential colleagues or even people who might work for you. These people may not be involved in detailed discussions, but will be asked whether you are a good fit. In meetings with them, you need to introduce yourself and give them enough detail so that they understand why you are qualified to do the job, but you should spend most of the time asking about them and the major challenges of their jobs. Their impression will then be of a team player who is interested in others.

You will also meet others incidentally, for example receptionists, telephone operators, administrators, even people at the coffee machine or in the cafeteria. Be nice to them, introduce yourself without pulling rank and ask in a light way about their favourite subject, themselves. For example, are they having a good day? If they are giving you a message, or showing you to the lift, thank them. Creating a positive impression never hurts and it can be surprising who you might need to ask to get a phone number or find a parking space.

The authors know of one technology company that always used a junior member of staff to take each candidate for lunch in the company canteen. Those who took the junior member of staff seriously stayed in the process, those who emphasised their own superiority were rejected. Yet another candidate was introduced to those who would work for him as the preferred candidate by the Chief Executive. The job was his to lose, and he lost it by being superior, overbearing and condescending. Each of the junior staff reported that they would find him difficult to work for.

Money and the package

'While money can't buy happiness, it certainly lets you choose your own form of misery'
Groucho Marx

You want a job for many reasons; one of these will be that you want to get paid. Ideally you would want to know exactly how much they might pay you if you get the job. For some jobs this is stated at the outset, but often the pay is either not stated or a range is given. You are trying to get the job, but not at any price. They are trying to get the right candidate, but also not at any price. There will be a zone of potential agreement where both the company and you are willing to strike a deal, but how to raise the subject without appearing too interested in money and reducing your chances?

94. Know what you want

It is important to be clear how much you will accept as a minimum. What is your 'walk away price' that you will not go below? If you are willing to work for a minimum wage then you need not worry, but for everyone else there is a minimum salary that they would be willing to accept. You need to know what the employer's range is so that you don't go through a long recruitment process only to turn down the job because it doesn't pay enough.

If you are moving from one job to another then your current pay package might be a good starting point, but the new job may also be a good opportunity to boost your earnings.

Having a clear walk away level will put you in a stronger negotiating position, if you are clear and confident your employer will see that you are serious and be more likely to agree to the right offer.

If you say nothing about pay during the interview process, the employer will offer what they think is a fair deal. You may not agree, but if you have said nothing you weaken your case.

95. Understand the policy or starting position

Your first step is to research the job and the organisation. If you are applying for a government-funded job, for example in a government department, the police, the military, or as a teacher then the pay will be determined by the grade. If it is not stated in the job information, make sure you find out the precise grade or level of the job and the current pay scales. This is public information and should be available from the organisation's Human Resources department.

Some large organisations also work on the same principle. In all cases it is worth contacting the HR department to ask. A good way to do this is to start by asking for any general conditions of employment or a copy of the employment contract. You can say you want to be prepared for your interviews. A reasonable follow-up question might then be an enquiry about the level or grade of the job and the associated pay scale.

If you have an interview with an HR person as part of the recruitment process, you can probe further. Many companies operate a recruitment process which starts with the hiring manager raising a job requisition. This is a form which describes the job, its grade or level and pay range. This requisition is then approved by various people so that everyone is clear that permission to hire has been given.

It is therefore reasonable to ask during an interview with an HR person, how the process works; if there is an open job requisition for this position and what the salary range is.

Another approach is to look for salary levels in equivalent jobs in other companies. You may draw a blank, but anything you can do to get advance information on the pay likely to be offered will considerably strengthen your hand.

Money and the package

96. Understand the total package

At some point you will be told what salary is being offered. It is important to understand the value of the total package of pay and benefits. In addition to basic pay there may be a performance-related part. In sales jobs this can often be up to 50% of the total pay or in some cases 100%. If there is a variable part make sure you understand exactly how it works. For example some sales plans may pay a basic and also quote OTE, 'On Target Earnings' for achieving a sales goal. The rules of the scheme will be documented and you must make sure you get a copy. You should ask what proportion of the current employed salespeople makes their OTE. You should look at the scheme to understand its structure. For example some OTE schemes pay nothing until 80% of the target is achieved; others might have a qualifying period and others may have a 'Draw' with claw-back. This means that you get paid a variable part in advance but if you fall short you have to pay it back.

For non-salespeople there may still be variable parts of the pay that depend on company profits or other more personal objectives. The principle is the same; make sure you know how it works.

Other important parts of a package might be a car, or car allowance; share options; medical cover, or company contribution to a pension scheme which can amount to 10% or more of salary. If the job has variable pay are benefits based on the total pay or just the fixed part? Make sure you understand these high-value items when assessing a package and seek clarification if you are not clear. Asking questions about pay and conditions is seen as being businesslike and organised. Only ask about the small number of significant items, do not spend time on small low-value benefits that will not affect your decision on whether to take the job. You can find out about those later.

97. Ask the right person for information in the right way.

During the recruitment process you will meet different types of people. Many of them will know something about the pay offered, but how and what you ask them will vary.

If you are dealing with an employment agency or a recruitment company, they will have been given information about the pay. In many cases they may have even advised the recruiting organisation about the pay levels in the market for the job in question. Therefore you can and should ask them directly what the pay and major benefits for the job are. They may answer with a range.

HR departments or other internal hiring groups should also know and can be asked directly. However you should not make a big deal of it and include pay and conditions in a list of other questions you might have.

It is important to find out who the 'hiring manager' is. This is the person who will make the final decision and will often be the person to whom the job reports. This person will know exactly what the pay is and how much flexibility there is. It is important that you raise this issue with the hiring manager. It indicates that you are serious about the job and is an entirely legitimate question.

You may meet others in the interview process; they could be colleagues, team leaders, or just someone who is used to assess candidates. Do not raise the issue of pay with them unless they raise it first. Often they will not know, but they might be interested because it gives them a perspective on their own salary. If in doubt politely avoid the issue with such people.

98. Ask about pay early

It is important to position your salary expectations early with the right people. There are several good reasons for talking about pay at an early stage:

- A. If you do not mention pay, then you could be wasting your time on a job that pays lower than you will accept.

- B. In any negotiation, it is always best to be negotiating around your 'stake in the ground' rather than theirs. If you mention pay early you have the initiative.

- C. There may be scope for increasing the level of pay on offer, if the hiring manager knows early that their original pay intention is too low. The further you get in the process the more difficult this will become.

Many candidates are concerned that talking about pay may be seen as rude or presumptive:

If I mention pay, they may think I am interested only in money. Pay should not be the first thing you mention but if you bring it up once you have demonstrated that you are the right person for the job and you are very enthusiastic about it, then it sounds perfectly natural. In fact, if you don't ask they may think you are not interested.

I may rule myself out by suggesting too high a figure. Assuming you have done your homework and chosen a pay figure that is right for you and reasonable for the job market, then you can do no harm. Companies do not choose the cheapest person for the job. They choose the best at a price they can afford. If they like you, but your price is too high, they will tell you. If the pay

Money and the package

they are offering is really below your 'walk away price' then it's better to know early.

When you mention pay it is sensible to do so in an indirect way. There are two approaches.

The first is based on your current earnings and you say: 'My current/last job paid a package of £40,000 per annum. I was hoping to improve on that.' Note that you use the word 'package'; this should include the value of everything you get in your best year or month. It needs to be close to the truth and you need to have the detail to hand. A good hiring manager will ask you how the package is made up.

The second approach uses third party information. For example: 'I have seen similar jobs paying from £40,000 per year'. Or more strongly: 'Similar jobs I have applied for are paying from £40,000 per year'. Only use this last phrasing if you are really in the process of applying for another job and have at least had an interview.

Mention pay in a mildly curious way, in the same way you might talk about which location you might be based in or what the start time might be. It's an important detail.

99. Understand the offer

If the interview is successful, you will be made an offer. This will usually happen first verbally and then in writing.

Verbal offers, even with a handshake, are good to get, but not worth anything. You should, of course, enthusiastically accept all verbal offers that you have even the slightest interest in accepting. **Do not do anything** on the basis of a verbal offer, in particular do not quit your existing job or make any commitments based on the assumption that you have got this one.

In response to a verbal offer you should clarify the important details, such as pay and start date, and write them down, so that the hiring manager can see that you recorded them.

If you do need to make a commitment, such as quit a job, ask the hiring person when you will get a formal written offer so that you can resign. This will be seen as a sign of commitment by the hiring manager that you are serious about taking the job.

When you do get the written offer, it may well be subject to references, a medical or other conditions. You should also get a cover letter setting out the pay and the rest of the package and your start date. You will also get a contract of employment and possibly other documents relating to important features of the pay package, like variable pay, pension, medical cover, share options and so forth.

Make sure you read all of this and understand it. Do not assume that because it comes from a company that it must be okay because all the existing employees have signed it.

Money and the package

For example:

There may be a probationary period during which you can be dismissed at short notice or there may be an assessment between the probationary period and full employment. Some benefits may not apply during a probationary period.

The package may include an element of variable pay or commission or bonus. If so, the rules should be explained to you. You need to check you understand how such pay is calculated and the rules for eligibility.

There may be restrictions on outside work or activities.

If you don't understand any of it, get some advice. In large companies the HR department will often be willing to explain these documents.

100. Negotiate the package

All packages are negotiable. Even in organisations with highly defined grade systems the pay package is negotiable, even if only to a small extent. The basic rule is that if you don't ask, you won't get. If you have got to the stage in the recruitment process where you are seriously talking about money then the employer wants you. As long as you ask in a respectful way then the employer will not change their mind because you asked for more.

Once you are in a company you will be subject to whatever rules govern pay increases for all existing staff and it will be much more difficult to negotiate significant increases in pay. Government-funded organisations will work on a system that involves grades or levels and increments within them. Large companies often work the same way. Usually there will be a company-wide upper limit on increases, so unless you are making a big jump within the organisation your pay increase will be determined by a well-defined set of rules. By skilful negotiation you might get a 10% improvement in the package, which in difficult economic times might easily be twice the amount you might get each year. So it's worth having a go. If you do it right there should be no downside, in fact you may look more attractive as a candidate.

Only negotiate with a person who has the authority to make (or request) a change, usually the hiring manager. That is one of the reasons you should raise pay at the first meeting with him or her. However, you may be fortunate enough to get a later meeting when details are finalised.

Money and the package

It is best to start your negotiation early with a positioning statement (see above); if you do this right, you won't have to negotiate because you will already have set a high bar. Once you receive a formal written offer it may be too late to negotiate, your pay may have been 'signed off' by a higher manager (see process section) and your bargaining becomes irritating and looks indecisive provoking the reaction 'Why didn't you mention this earlier?'

You must always link your negotiation to your commitment to the job. Rather than just ask for more or say directly that the offer is unattractive, it is best to state your negotiation as a personal reaction. In particular never use the word 'you' as in 'the offer *you* have made'. It sounds like an accusation and will invoke an emotional defensive response, better to say either 'the company' as in 'The offer the company has made' or 'We', see below. Finally, be specific about the salary you were hoping to get.

Putting this all together you might say:

'I am really excited about the job and I'm looking forward to being part of the team, however I was hoping for a slightly higher salary. My expectations were for something around £45,000.'

This phrasing will allow the hiring manager to give a reaction. It may be positive, or they may just say that this is the final offer, in which case you have lost nothing.

Whatever the response, unless it is a direct question, let the matter drop for now. It is likely that they will need to think about this, or see what they can do within a budget or other restriction. You have made your reaction clear; now move on to other topics.

Remember that it is not just basic pay that is negotiable, you may want to negotiate start date, or in radical circumstances the nature of your employment, for example working as a contractor rather than an employee. In smaller more flexible organisations, you may be able to negotiate working hours or vacation.

Money and the package

101. Use multiple offers carefully

If you are lucky enough to get more than one job offer you must play your hand carefully. Do it wrong and you could lose both.

First, be clear about the status of each offer. If they are verbal offers they are not real. They may be highly likely to happen, but they are not a firm commitment.

You must be clear about which job you would prefer. Don't think, 'OK I'll just see which one I get', make a positive choice. In both these examples we assume that Job A is offered first, but you then have a final interview for Job B.

Job A is best

You have an offer for Job A (which you prefer) and then get a final interview for Job B. If job A is the one you want and you get a written offer, take it and cancel Job B. If the Job A offer was verbal then don't say anything about it in your interview with Job B. If you get a verbal offer for Job B, you can then enquire about when you might get the written offer. By not saying anything you allow the people at Job A more time to get their written offer out. You then wait for both written offers and take Job A if you get that, otherwise you take Job B.

Job B is best

If you are holding any sort of offer from Job A, but you'd prefer Job B: you mention it in an open and honest way to the people at company B. If you don't, the people of company B will not know that there is some urgency and the decision process may go on so long that you are forced either to take Job A or let the Job A offer lapse. If the company B people know your position and really want you, then they will try to meet your time constraints.

Under either scenario, do not reject any offer until you have an alternative offer in writing.

102. Don't be greedy

In the points above we have talked about the importance of knowing what you want and opportunities for negotiation and managing offers. However, don't be too greedy. Throughout the interview process you will have displayed a positive enthusiastic attitude, demonstrating that you really want the job. Asking for the right salary demonstrates many positive qualities about you: it shows self-confidence and the ability to stand up for your point of view. Most employers value these qualities at all levels. They assume that if you stand up for what is right now, you will do the same as an employee. There is, however, a fine line between defending your right to be paid a reasonable salary and overt self-interest. You must always maintain a cooperative spirit, if a negotiation becomes adversarial, then you have lost. You will either not get the money you want or not get the job.

In a negotiation, the more power you have the more likely you are to get what you want. In most job hiring processes power is unequal, the employer probably has multiple candidates, but you may have fewer job opportunities. However, employers will not be making their decision only on price. They will choose who they believe to be the best candidate that fits their budget. If you suggest a salary they cannot afford and they explain they have an upper budgetary limit, you need to accept this reason as valid. You can give them more space by not responding, but if you push too hard you lose the job, not because you are too expensive but because you are seen as too self-centred. This is not an argument for avoiding negotiation, done right it is entirely positive, but it must be kept within a positive, cooperative spirit that recognises that when you join, you will be working to support the company, not just for yourself.

103. Be open, but at the right time

There may be things you need from a job, which you don't want to mention, just in case it reduces your chances of being offered that job. You may have some commitments, such as booked holiday, or a need to finish early on a particular day of the week to take care of a family commitment. In general, permanent issues need to be mentioned early, but temporary ones can be delayed.

If you are a single parent and this affects the hours you can work, then you need to mention this early, because it might breach a specific requirement of the job. A good way to mention something like that is to flag the issue at the first meeting, but only mention the specific implications later or if asked directly. So in this example you might mention in passing that you are a single parent in the first meeting, but talk about your need for flexibility later. You must, however, say something, failure to mention a specific significant issue early will be seen as dishonest. Making a full revelation too early may rule you out before you have had a chance to let them see what a great asset to the company you are.

Often, a good time to raise these issues in more detail is when you meet the hiring manager for the second time. You need to be raising this issue with the person who has the authority to vary the job requirements to meet your needs.

If the issue is temporary, such as a booked holiday, or a wedding, then it is a detail and it does not affect your fundamental suitability for the job. Raising it too early is not material and suggests that you are thinking too much about

Money and the package

yourself and not enough about the job. You must still raise it, but not until late in the process.

Whatever the issue, if you do not raise it, or raise it too late, you may turn something that could have been managed into an unforeseen iceberg and created distrust.

Closing thoughts

We hope you have found the book useful and that it has given you some fresh ideas and inspiration. Once you have read the book you should find it a useful and easy to use reference and memory prompt to keep you focussed on being productive through your job hunt.

The book is based on a few simple principles which can be distilled to:

1. Prepare: make sure you know yourself, what jobs you want and where to find them. Research companies and practise interviews.

2. Focus: spend your time and effort on those activities that are important.

3. Take action: getting a job requires you to be active and tenacious. It's a competitive world out there and those job applicants who act will beat those who wait.

4. Be determined and patient: don't expect instant results and keep up your level of activity over a sustained period of time. It's a marathon, not a sprint.

5. Do it well: whether it's your CV, application letter or interview technique, spend time to do it well.

Throughout your working life you should continually be alert for fresh opportunities and ways to enhance your skills, career and job options. This does not mean you need to change jobs all the

Closing thoughts

time but it does mean using the techniques in this book to understand the opportunities you encounter.

If you do need to make a move now or in the future, remember that job hunting is a competitive process and that employers will invariably hire an enthusiastic and positive person over someone who is not. Enjoy your job hunting; be disciplined, organised and tenacious, inject a little humour and fun and you will succeed and reap benefits throughout your career.

Best of luck and have a great career!

About the authors

Max Dobres is cofounder of Bookham Consulting Associates. He has an MSc in Psychology and has held VP and executive positions in Europe and the US for leading global corporations. Max is also a non-executive director and adviser to smaller organisations. He has reviewed and interviewed thousands of applicants and trained other managers on how to conduct selection processes. He has even been on the interview board for Blue Badge London Tourist Guides. In this book he tells you what you need to do to get to the front of the job queue, how to do it and some common mistakes to avoid.

Mark Hennessy is the founder of Objective Professional Services. He has over 20 years experience in Executive Recruitment, team building and HR consulting specifically for early stage technology and services firms across Europe. He has run his own business since 1994. His interest in building early stage businesses has led Mark to become involved with numerous fledgling companies, assisting them with planning, identifying funding options, building sales strategies and hiring. He is also a mentor within SetSquared – the technology spinout incubator for Bristol, Bath, Southampton and Surrey Universities.

Between them the authors have reviewed tens of thousands of CVs and interviewed thousands of clients for hundreds of jobs.

About the authors

Bookham Consulting Associates

Bookham Consulting Associates provides a rapid structured approach and practical support to help companies solve key problems of market expansion and growth.

Bookham Consulting Associates offers individual executive coaching and corporate coaching of groups to ensure that executives are equipped to face the changing requirements of organisations and markets.

www.bookhamconsulting.com

Objective Professional Services

Objective Professional Services is one of the leading recruitment firms specialising in building early stage software companies. It also runs major programmes for more mature businesses.

It has a track record second to none and is widely respected for its commitment to long-term relationships, integrity, service, delivery and team building.

www.objectiveps.com

Get a Job

This book is available electronically for the Kindle from Amazon.

Hard copies of the book are available from most good booksellers or directly from: www.createspace.com